Liberia: Window of time 1948-50

A snapshot of the life of a mining engineeer

 www.trafford.com

North America & international
toll-free: 844-688-6899 (USA & Canada)
fax: 812 355 4082

LIBERIA
WINDOW OF TIME
1948 - 1950

Ir. Albert Reilingh, *m.i.*

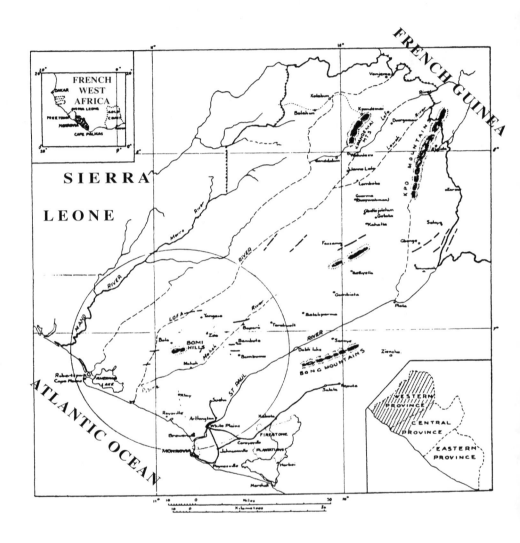

1948 map of the Western Province, Liberia

Introduction

In my first job after university I was exposed to unusual circumstances, many of which I had forgotten until recently when I received a bundle of letters, which I had written during my first job in Liberia. My mother had saved those letters. Without these it would have been impossible to recollect what happened. Memories came alive and inspired me to write the story of my experiences as a mining engineer in Liberia.

My formative years at the Delft University in Holland, starting in 1938, had been turbulent. In 1939 I was conscripted into the Dutch army due to the Second World War. My only action was shooting at Junker transport planes that dropped parachutists around The Hague. Ironically, it was the same type of plane that transported me to Liberia nine years later. The Germans overran Holland and after the bombing of Rotterdam in 1940, the Dutch army capitulated. The Germans figured that the Dutch were their blood-brothers and disbanded the army; only the professional soldiers were interned into prisoner-of-war camps. I returned to my studies. As a student in an occupied country, I became involved politically as well as illegally. In early 1943, when Stalingrad fell, the Germans were livid and ordered all previous army personnel and all able men over eighteen years old—including all university students who refused to sign loyalty to the Germans—to report for work in Germany. I had to go into hiding. This was the second interruption in my studies and it lasted until the end of the war. When the war was over in 1945, I wanted freedom, but I felt responsible to assist in the rebuilding of Holland. I had to finish my studies. This took another two years and by that time I was 28 years old.

I had to decide what career path to follow. The oil companies did not appeal to me. The coal mines in Holland, although modern, seemed too close to home. Holland still had the Dutch East Indies with mining of tin, coal and gold. During the transition period from the Dutch East Indies to Indonesia, I figured that we, Dutch especially, should not force ourselves onto this country. We should have the patience to wait until we were invited back, a similar feeling as I had experienced toward the Germans. Realizing this, I figured that in my life time we would never be invited back to Indonesia.

Two positions for mining engineer and geologist in Liberia became available at the end of 1947. It looked challenging and I applied. The general manager of the Liberia Mining Company visited Holland and I was hired three months before I had completed my university studies. Also hired was a just graduated mining engineer, Theo Immink, who I knew casually.

The only thing about Liberia I knew was that the country was somewhere on the west coast of Africa. I had to find out more.

In the nineteenth century, after slavery was abolished in the U.S., eighteen thousand black freemen settled on the coast of West Africa in the period 1822-46, between the British and the French colonial influences. These men, later called Americano-Liberians, carved out a country between British Sierra Leone and the French Ivory Coast, which they called Liberia. They declared it a republic in 1846. It would have been crushed by the local tribes or these colonial powers, were it not for the support of the U.S. government and the then U.S. President James Monroe. At last in 1919, after the French had annexed a chunk of the claimed territory, the boundaries were clearly established and surveyed.

The coast was uninviting as there were no natural harbours. This fact made the interior inaccessible. The climate was tropical, hot and humid, with two seasons, a dry one and a wet one. It was economically one of the poorest countries on the African continent. In 1926 Liberia was financially bailed out by the Firestone Rubber Company, which acquired a concession for a rubber plantation. A gravel road was built from the plantation to Monrovia and to the airport at Robertsville. Monrovia, the capital, became the main trading centre.

The Christian, English-speaking Americano-Liberians formed the upper crust in the country. There were at least eight major tribes, some pushed from the coast by these settlers. These tribes were pagan, except for the Madingos in the north-west, who were Muslim. Besides a Lutheran mission in the north-west and a Catholic mission in the south-east, there were quite a number of Christian missions mainly from the U.S., throughout the country.

In the 1930s, iron ore was discovered 75 kilometres inland. During the Second World War, Liberia became strategically important to the

U.S., being the only country in West Africa outside French and British influences. In 1943 the currency changed from the pound to the dollar. The airport was upgraded and an all-weather road was built to French Guinea. A harbour, a power plant and a bridge over the St. Paul River were promised by the U.S. government as economic stimulation.

President Wm. V. S. Tubman, elected in 1943, was the first native Liberian to be president and he endeavoured to open up the country and to eliminate the differences between the tribes. The Liberian constitution stipulated that only black men could be citizens. It was guessed that the population was around 1.5 million, living in an area a little smaller than three times The Netherlands or about equal to Pennsylvania.

In 1945, the Liberia Mining Company was established.

This little information was all there was available. It was the unknown that appealed to me.

In the first week of January 1948, I left Holland by K.L.M. to Paris for an overnight stop. I continued with Air France to Dakar and from there on a Junker, an airplane that the French apparently had confiscated from the Germans. The Junker was a war-time trimotor transport plane with corrugated steel plates as a skin. Between the vertical and the horizontal walls there were sizeable openings in the body, so that between the seats I could sometimes see canoes with two or three black fishermen on the ocean below. From my window seat there was no land in sight.

Flying over the ocean I had to think of the German parachutists in 1940, who like me with their dreams for the future, were sneaked over Holland and dropped into an inhospitable country. How would I fare?

The first stop was Conakry, Sierra Leone. The airport terminal was a mud hut with a corrugated roof, a few tables and some chairs standing outside. Chickens were running around pecking for their food. It looked quite messy to me coming from a neat country like Holland. There was not enough room to sit at the terminal, so most of the passengers stood perspiring in the only other shade at the airport, under the wing of our plane. As soon as the plane was airborne, the temperature dropped and I perspired no more.

The next stop, about an hour later, was Robertsville International Airport in Liberia. Coming out of the plane the heat engulfed me again and then, for the first time, I realized that this was the environment that I would be working and living in. The heat was tiring and I was glad to be picked up by a company car to go to Monrovia. During the ride from the airport, I experienced cultural shock. Everybody I saw was black and the people wore few or no clothes. The houses were all mud huts, the roads were unpaved and it was dusty. All these new impressions hit me. I had arrived in the heart of Africa.

Two days later Theo Immink arrived. His experiences included a fire sputtering engine and an emergency landing in Agadir, south Morocco, with a change of plane.

We were going to work together in exploration.

The Expedition to Bomi Hills

The introduction to the jungle was an experience so different from what Theo and I were used to. Many situations could go wrong. Through our optimism we were fortunate enough to somehow handle these. But it was a learning experience for which we were not prepared.

The general manager told us first to visit Bomi Hills and make ourselves acquainted with its type of iron-ore deposit, before striking out.

In Monrovia we were introduced to an old-timer, Jordense, to get us started on our first expedition. Jordense, a phlegmatic, middle-aged Dutchman, tall, blond with blue eyes, had lived in Liberia for some twenty years and seemed to be absorbed by this country. His movements and speech were slow, he knew how to manipulate people and he had one hundred percent use of the only company car. He knew the habits of the local people, their businesses and government positions. As representative of the company, he was able to steer favors to whoever he needed a favor from in return. That way he made himself appealing and important, and this he wanted us to be aware of. Jordense introduced us to our local company staff. He guided us to receive resident status, registered us at the Dutch consulate and introduced us to the company doctor, who checked our inoculations and supplied us with a box with medicines for our expedition.

We drove to the shopping center along the Waterstreet, in the heart of the city. The stores were extremely long warehouses, with a counter along the street and docks on the waterfront for loading and unloading the barges. Coming from Europe, where at that time stores were almost empty and most of the supplies were rationed piecemeal and still on coupons, we were surprised to find coffee, tea, cigarettes, cigars, canned food and clothing readily available. Because our company had a line of credit, we, as white men of the company, were allowed to swing our legs over the counter and help ourselves to the necessary food and material. Jordense made sure that we got the right supplies for the month-long expedition to the Interior. We had no idea what was required, which ended up being much more than we thought. These supplies were piled on the counter.

Jordense told us to crate the supplies in boxes weighing not more than twenty kilograms, the maximum a man could be expected to carry eight hours a day. While we crated the supplies, Jordense hired our crew. We ended up with some thirty men, including an overseer, who could speak and write English, a cook and a steward. On the fourth and last day we picked up the expedition money. Liberian labour law required that the company employees be paid weekly. We needed more than a thousand U.S. dollars in copper, nickel and silver coins. This amounted to quite some weight.

Now we were ready to go on our expedition.

The next day, early in the morning, our crew waited at the gate. The overseer was the only one with boots and a trunk for his belongings. The men had no luggage and no footwear. They wore their clothing, a pair of short trousers and a singlet, a kind of undershirt.

Our company truck came to the company guest-house. We all got on, Theo and I sitting on the front seat beside the driver and the thirty-man crew standing in the back of the truck. At the Waterstreet stores we picked up the boxes of supplies and the tools. Then we drove to the crossing at the St. Paul River, about fifteen kilometres north of Monrovia. There we crossed in a canoe, fashioned from a hollowed-out tree. Each crossing took more than half an hour. In all, we were ferrying from before noon until late afternoon. On the other side, another company truck transported us some five kilometres farther north to Brewerville. Here, Theo and I stayed overnight in the company guest-house.

Canoe crossing at the St. Paul River

From Brewerville it was two days on foot to Bomi Hills. We were so green, but we had received lots of advice from Jordense. Once en route, we quickly realized, that we were on our own and left to our own devices. An old army truck would take us to the end of the completed road. Our first stop was the Kpo River. Here our carpenters had built a pontoon ferry, using empty-sealed, 45-gallon drums for buoyancy. A hand-operated winch was bolted on top and the end of the rope was anchored across the river. This ferry was far from stable and for safety, we crossed the truck first without anybody on it. When the truck drove onto the pontoon, it tipped badly, but the pontoon straightened out because its front end settled on the shallow river bottom. It was a top-heavy situation and in the middle of the river, where the current was strong, we had some anxious moments when the ferry tipped dangerously from side to side. We could have lost all our supplies then and there. After the truck was safely landed, we crossed with the crew. Then we trucked to where the road ended and the forest began. There the truck was unloaded and left us. Theo and I split up the loads for the crew and we started walking the trail leading to Bomi Hills, followed by the carriers, who carried the loads on their heads.

We reached Clay, a district town of some three hundred huts, half-way between Brewerville and Bomi Hills, where we spent our first night. Our overseer had arranged with the town chief for our carriers to lodge with the townspeople and he issued them food from our supplies. Theo and I could stay in the palaver house, a sort of council house in the middle of the town, which was open on all sides and close to the headquarters of the district commissioner. The town chief and the clan chief came to pay their respects. They had come to size us up and to see if they could get something to smoke. After a short introduction they left. We heard from our overseer that the chiefs were elected by the local tribes. He also explained that the major town in the district became known as district town and the central government dispatched a commissioner there with a small contingent of soldiers. The commissioner seemed to have the final say in all matters and the power to enforce his decisions.

We had walked four hours in the tropical heat and were perspiring profusely. Our steward prepared a bucket filled with water for each of us and laid out our dry clothing. It was behind some huts, but visible to all the natives in town. Because our white bodies were strange to them, they stood around and watched us with curiosity. Being surrounded by people, especially women wearing only a wrap around their lower half and nothing on top, was a surprising situation. It took time to get used to this.

Our steward set up chairs and a folding bridge table in the town square in front of the palaver house and we settled down to relax. The day turned into night, the transition taking only about half an hour. Our steward brought a kerosene lamp from our kitchen across the square and he promoted a towel to serve as a tablecloth. Within an hour our cook had the meal ready: chicken soup, rice with chicken, and a hot drink. I did not realize it then, but for the next two years, this same meal would be our mainstay. All these arrangements were apparently customary to our cook and steward, but pleasantly new to us.

During the meal, we heard a shot in the bush some distance away. A little later we heard another shot, then another and another, all the time getting closer and closer. After some ten minutes, and lots of shots around us, a troop of some twenty soldiers marched into the square. In the middle were four men carrying a hammock with the district commissioner resting in it. Theo and I decided to act as if nothing surprised us and continued our meal undisturbed, though we were amazed at this show. Half an hour later, a soldier came over and said that the district commissioner would like to meet us. After dinner we went over to the district commissioner's compound and introduced ourselves. The commissioner seemed a pleasant, well-educated official. We did not know what to talk about, so Theo and I told him of our plans to leave the next day for Bomi Hills. The town chief joined us and asked if he could show us around town. There were lots of huts, which looked all the same to me. I was tired and I left Theo the honour of being the guest of the town chief. I slipped back to the palaver house, undressed and crawled into my army cot, rigged with mosquito netting, where in full view of the population, I fell asleep.

The next morning the cook had prepared tea with breakfast, which was a surprise to us. In Holland, as a student I had lived on a shoestring budget and during the war, food had become scarce. Coffee and tea were non-existent and I was used to having a glass of water at breakfast. Now, here in the jungle, we were served our breakfast in relative luxury.

We said good-bye to the town chief and the clan chief and gave them their *dash*—money to be distributed among the people who had helped us with lodgings—. We said good-bye to the district commissioner and continued on our way.

That afternoon we arrived at Bomi Hills. For two days we had walked through the bush over a winding, hemmed-in trail with virtually no visibility. The only clearings were the few villages and the town of Clay. Now we came to the mine site clearing. To the north, I could see a mountain rising far above the surrounding countryside and even higher on the west side, which was called Monkey Hill. It was an imposing view. I realized that was the overgrown iron-ore outcrop, Bomi Hills.

Bomi Hills outcrop deforested a year later

During the next few weeks Theo and I familiarized ourselves with the iron-ore outcrop. Using our crew to make trails and clear areas for observation, we noted the structure of the host formation and the intrusion of the ore with the faults, measuring the thickness and the extent of the ore body. We took samples of the different types of ore and estimated the tonnage. It gave us a good understanding of how to evaluate other iron deposits.

We would start working early in the morning at six and by ten o'clock be soaking wet because of the intense heat. We were very thirsty and decided to take buckets of water with us to the worksite. Drinking all this water caused us to sweat even more, getting wet earlier and making us feel languid sooner. The salty sweat attracted mosquitoes in hordes. Around noon we took a break. Our cook had made sandwiches for lunch and the water carriers stood around us, watching with hungry eyes. We started to give away sandwiches, but pretty soon the whole crew was standing around us looking hungry. It was impossible to satisfy that many people, so it was easier to skip lunch. From then on I had only two meals a day. The tropical heat persisted and I felt constantly tired.

The first time I walked alone in the bush, I was startled by a very long, green-spotted, arm-thick snake slithering through the branches just in front of my face. After that, for safety, I always had a man walk in front of me carrying a cutlass with a blade the length of an arm. The locals were much more aware of what to watch for in the jungle. At the camp, I saw a native kill a snake which was too close to his child. He cut off the head, put a stick through the mouth and then drove the stick into the ground, so that the venom could not hurt anybody. That was their safety factor. The snake's body continued to jerk for a long time, so he stopped that by cutting a little piece from the tail. Then the snake's body moved no longer.

These first weeks were a good time for Theo and me to get to know each other better. We had studied about the same time, but our paths had seldom crossed, except over the last two years. Theo was three years older, had married two years before we went to Liberia and had a son. When Theo signed up with the Liberia Mining Company, he was promised that his wife, Cor, could follow him within six months. Theo was tall, broad-shouldered, and he towered above the local crew. He was a good walker, but not a real athlete. Theo had a sense of fair play and a very good sense of humor. He readily changed his thinking to the different circumstances. One of the water carriers did not understand him when he said "Wait a minute," so he changed his instruction to, "Wait small," and that worked. He could see the amusing side of situations. One of the men told Theo, that he had been a dispatcher in the British army in India during the war "on a prrrt-prrrt," indicating at the same time the starting of a motorcycle, Theo repeated: "On a prrt-prrt?" and after that he called the man Tamba Motorcycle. The man liked that so much that from that day on, his last name was Motorcycle. Theo was an optimistic, capable and conscientious worker. We were able to support each other when the need occurred. My friendship extended to his wife, Cor, and has lasted over fifty years.

When we first arrived in Bomi Hills, the local superintendent Beuken had assigned us a mud hut. We enjoyed living in this mud hut, as it was quite comfortable and better than a tent.

There was a sizable porch serving as living room, a kitchen, a room for bathing and a bedroom, all under one roof. No windows were required. This hut had a cement floor and the walls were cement-coated on the inside and white-washed inside and outside. The porch had a mud railing, which was also cement-coated. The ceilings were made of woven straw. The roof was thatched with a thick layer of palm leaves, making the huts waterproof. It was cooler in the porch living room than outside and it was here that we had our meals and spent our leisure times during the evenings and on Sundays.

Relaxing on the porch in Bomi Hills

We often visited the superintendent Beuken, a one-track minded man, who could be a hard-nosed task master. Modern tools and equipment were still not available to him. With unskilled labour and only picks, shovels, axes, cutlasses and saws—using vines as ropes and sticks as survey poles—he was building roads and clearing the outcrop. Using local building customs he had built the two mud huts and when enough planks were sawed, he had built the two bungalows. Also a banana farm was started. The Bomi Hills compound had no fencing and no gate.

We did not like Beuken's unbending strictness and his lack of consideration for the local people. He seemed a real colonial of the nineteenth century. He told us about his experiences in the Dutch East Indies, where he had worked before the war. But he gave us many practical hints. He was amused with our water problem and suggested a better way of handling it. One canteen of water had to last until the end of the shift. Upon returning home we were to drink four or five glasses of water to perspire and stay hydrated, then take a hot bath, as hot as one could stand. Afterwards, the afternoon felt pleasantly cool. We asked where we could find a bath. He suggested our wash tub. At first, when we heard this, we thought, "A hot bath?" However, after trying this, it really was the way to go and I had my hot bath whenever possible. Later on, we had a canvas bucket with a spout in the bottom that our steward could hang from a branch. With an attached string we could control the flow of water from the spout and be able to take a real shower.

Beuken had moved into one of the bungalows. He told us that the second bungalow was for the Immink family. His and Theo's wives were expected to arrive in the next few months. The smaller mud hut became my home. The bigger mud hut was a hotel for four guests. Beuken's cook and steward provided the required services. If the hotel was filled, the overflow was put in an extra cot in my bedroom.

A small village to house the local labour force was being built a good distance east along a creek and our crew stayed there.

It took us three weeks to complete the re-evaluation of the ore-body.

When we were sure we had a grasp of the situation, we returned to Monrovia. On the way back we analyzed how to improve the expedition and identified three major problems.

Firstly, the labour situation was unsatisfactory. Labour problems among the carriers from the different tribes—each with its own customs—caused constant friction. The majority of our crew was Bussy. Since it seemed to be the easiest tribe to get along with, we decided to endeavour to get men from this tribe only.

Secondly, we had a constant problem with our money. Jordense had told us to divide the cash into several locked boxes in order to reduce the risk of losing it all. To control where the money was, we had made lists of the amounts and location. As we were not bookkeepers, we did not keep a daily tab on our money issues and we were recording from memory. We made mistakes and the administration became time-consuming and confusing. We ended up not knowing where the money was, nor where the keys for these boxes were. Theo came up with a simple solution. We put all the money into one box and told everybody that the whole crew was responsible for that box: if we lost it, nobody would be paid. We also assigned one carrier to look after that box. This solved our problem: we never lost any money and our administration was simplified.

Thirdly, as we had to hire and fire employees on the spot, we needed guidance as to appropriate compensation. At the Firestone plantation, at that time the biggest employer in the country, the basic wage was eighteen cents a day. These wages had been established before the war and not changed since. The Firestone stores had never increased their pricing, so the buying power had remained constant. Employees were also supplied with a hut and medical care. Our company used thirty-two cents a day as the base rate. On our expeditions we also paid our carriers for their food and lodgings, as well as a travel allowance of four cents a day. This was attractive enough to draw people to apply for this job. At that time rice was one cent per pound and bananas eight for a penny.

After discussing these three points, Theo and I decided to do the preparations for the following expedition ourselves. We reached Monrovia and paid off the crew, thus completing our first expedition. We reported to the head office.

We spent a week in Monrovia and this time in the office we heard stories about the Liberia Mining Company and its unexpected incorporation in 1945. In the early 1930s, the West African Company—a Dutch owned trading company—had sent out a mining engineer to look for gold deposits. He discovered the Bomi Hills iron deposit around 1936. A consortium was formed with Dutch and German mining interests to finance the diamond drilling in 1937. By 1938, a high-grade ore body of sufficient size to be economically developed was established. In 1939, the Second World War interfered and the development was put on hold. The property lay dormant. When Liberia declared war on Germany in 1944, the property was confiscated. In 1945, a colonel in the U.S. army on his way through West Africa heard about this ore body. Being a millionaire and an entrepreneur, he acquired the exploitation rights, as well as additional exploration rights within a radius of fifty kilometres. To further develop the iron deposit, he engaged the interest and know-how of Mueller and Co of Rotterdam, the Dutch company that had been involved in this iron-ore project before the war.

By 1948 the company had a head office and a guest-house in Monrovia.

The head office was a three-storey mansion. The main floor was for office workers, the assistant manager lived with his wife on the top floor, the basement held the laundry room and the waiting room for the dispatchers. The guest-house was a similar mansion, unattractive on the outside, but luxurious inside with a large dining room and ten bedrooms. The hall and the stairs had gorgeous waxed, shiny, deep-coloured mahogany floors and walls. There were six stewards and two cooks to serve the guests. Both buildings had twenty-four-hour watchmen services.

Company guest-house, Monrovia

We were soon able to reorient ourselves in town: a typical bustling, messy African trading port with West European and Middle Eastern traders, their stores and bazaars. After being in the jungle, I found it an attractive, lively settlement. The city, with perhaps thirty thousand inhabitants, was well planned with broad gravel streets at right angles to one another. It was quite dusty. Driving through town to the waterfront shopping center Jordense and I passed the palace of Liberian President Wm. V. S. Tubman on Ashmun Street. It was located on the only paved street block in the country and thus free from dust. To limit noise, cars were not permitted to toot their horns here. On top of this, jeeps and trucks were not allowed to drive in front of the palace. All of this was to improve the prestige of the Office of the President.

Elsewhere in town, the few cars constantly blew their horns to clear paths, as people did not restrict themselves to the sidewalks. In the centre of every major intersection, a policeman sat atop an on-end, 45-gallon drum. Between his legs, through a hole in the top of the drum, was a long pole with the signs of STOP and GO, perpendicular to each other, sticking high in the air. There were usually people standing around this policeman, talking. He felt like a very important man and he would forget the position of the sign. If a car approached and the sign read STOP, the car would blow its horn to get the policeman's attention, so he would turn the pole. If two cars arrived at the same time from different directions, the one that tooted the loudest had the best chance of getting the right of way. The drivers were responsible for making sure that it was safe to proceed.

The town was divided into three sections. In the west part, on the high outcrop that formed a peninsula in the Atlantic, were the big, upscale houses, many occupied by Americano-Liberians, government officials, embassy staffs, professional people and traders. At night there was a nice, cool sea-breeze, making it a favoured spot for an evening drive.

In the middle part of town was the business section with government buildings, the bank and, along the River Masurado, many trading companies with their warehouses and shops.

The east side was where the local population lived. At the far end of town the houses changed to mud huts and these were scattered and unorganized, similar to an interior village.

The capital, and for that matter the entire country, had to import all its goods and services from abroad by sea. The freighters, which brought people as well as the supplies, were anchored one kilometer out in open sea. They took more than a week to unload their freight with the local barges shuttling between Waterstreet stores and the ships.

Waterstreet's shopping centre, Monrovia

We were busy getting new supplies in town. Of course we needed to get our first-aid kit back up to par. Before we left on our initial expedition, our company doctor had supplied us with a box of medicines. On the bottles were written the symptoms of the sickness and the doses to be used. During the expedition we had dispensed medicines at the end of the day. One evening, after our first-aid session, Theo and I decided to check out the medicine kit. There were some bottles with antivenom for snakebite. Instructions were based on the acidity of the snake's venom. We had no knowledge of snakes, nor their venom's acidity. We did not even have the capability to check this. These serums were useless to us. In case of a snake bite, we would probably be forced to rely on the local witch doctor.

On the return from our expedition, I had sent the medicine box to the doctor's office to be replenished.The next day I was urgently called to the doctor's office. Before any conversation started, a nurse told me to pull down my pants and gave me an injection in my hip. I did not know why, until the doctor asked me how I had gotten syphilis. Theo had used up all the venereal disease medicines for the treatment of our headman, but the doctor assumed that one of us had the disease. I was quick to correct him, explaining that it was our headman who needed that medicine. He examined me thoroughly to make sure I was telling him the truth. Then he lectured me, saying he had been contracted by the company to provide medical services for staff only and that the medicines were not meant for my crew.

Regardless Theo and I supplied our crew with the medicines, whenever we had them. We found that the usual problems on an expedition were a sore back from too heavy a load and or too rough a trail, an infected foot from a neglected cut in the sole, or venereal disease.

After taking care of our supplies, the hiring of a crew was our next concern. Most of our carriers had disappeared. We endeavoured to get the good ones back. There was no chance to hire men in Bomi Hills, we had to find them in Monrovia. We could not afford to have men sick or disabled; we had to check the soles of their feet. We also wanted strong and intelligent carriers, so we developed a test. Two poles, longer than the tallest man, were pushed into the ground a short distance apart and a connecting pole was tied across the top. We asked the men to climb the pole and cut the high horizontal pole in the middle. Of course, this was an impossible situation and they would hurt themselves doing this. The ones who grabbed the saw anxiously and wanted to start cutting immediately, lacked common sense. We put them to one side. We figured that the other ones, who looked at the situation with apprehension and hesitation, were the thinkers. We put them to the other side. When we had all the carriers we needed in the group that hesitated, we asked them to come to the office. Our male nurse checked them for venereal disease and cuts in their soles. If they passed inspection, they became part of our crew.

Theo and I discussed with Jordense the need for an interpreter. We had heard that in the Interior, there were twenty-eight languages and dialects. A good interpreter was hard to find and having to hire a specialist meant burdening the expedition, because this man would require a personal steward and an extra carrier for his trunk. Jordense had been smart to hire an overseer who was able to serve as interpreter for our first expedition. We intended to arrange this again.

Our first overseer had taught us about the politeness of the people in the Interior. It was their custom to agree with a stranger. I would ask someone at a road crossing, "Is this road going to the town of Bopolo?" The locals would always say, "Yes" and I could end up in the wrong town. Instead my question had to be phrased, "Where does this road go?" To confirm the answer, I would also ask where the other road led.

The language barrier made it impossible for me to communicate directly with the local population, so simple problems had led to big misunderstandings. We had labour problems the first day, when we travelled from Brewersville to Clay. We travelled on the company truck to the end of the completed section of the road and after unloading the truck, we told the carriers to each take a load. That did not work, as each man took a box that looked light and about half of the materials and supplies were left. Instead of letting our overseer solve that problem, we figured that we had better get the expedition moving and so divided the balance of the material as we saw fit. Some carriers argued and were reluctant to take their loads. It seemed that we were heading towards a revolt, but when we moved on, the men followed.

An hour or so later, the men complained to me, "Oh boh, a happy loa....!" My reaction was to say with enthusiasm, "Yes, happy load!" That afternoon, when we reached our destination, these same men asked for liniment to soothe their strained muscles and I slowly realized that I had misunderstood them. What they were trying to say was, "Oh boss, a *heavy* load." But they could not pronounce the *v* and instead used the *p*. This pronounciation problem mushroomed into the labour problem.

To get a job the men realized that there was an advantage if one had some rudimentary knowledge of English. They picked up the sound and the meaning of words from foreigners on the job. But these foreigners were not all versed in English, as in my case, where I had a heavy Dutch accent. This resulted in using only half of a word as they heard it. "A big hill" was heard and pronounced as "uh bi hi." This simplification was also used in the names of settlements. All were referred to as "ton" and this could mean anywhere from three to over three thousand huts. We learned some of their vocabulary: "palaver", a pidgin word, was used daily. It meant to talk or discuss and each town had its palaver house. "Dash" was the word for tipping, but it could also mean a bribe. Sometimes there was a vocabulary problem. For instance, the local language had no word for parking a car, but this was solved imaginatively: "Where car sleep?"

That week in Monrovia we secured our supplies. We piled them on counters, scrounged for empty boxes and crated them. We also were fortunate to hire a group of solid men, who became the core of our work party. We picked up the money for the expedition from the office. After making these arrangements, we returned with the new crew to Bomi Hills. We were ready for the exploration of the hinterland.

We thought we were becoming pros.

The First Expedition in the Concession

The evening before our departure from Bomi Hills, we discussed the upcoming expedition with superintendent Beuken. We felt quite confident and optimistic, but the first day of this expedition turned out to be a real calamity.

Our concession was limited to a fifty-kilometre radius around Bomi Hills. The north-western part was delineated by the Mano River, which was the border with Sierra Leone. The south-western section bordered the Atlantic Ocean. The St. Paul River was just inside the south-eastern section and east of this sector was the Firestone plantation. The topographical maps of the Firestone plantation and the clearings in the countryside gave us a good insight into the configuration of the coastal area. The north-eastern section was unknown.

The coast was flat with dunes and swamps, stabilized by two main outcrops: in the west at Roberts Port and in the east at Monrovia. The area directly behind the coastline had mangrove forests, where we did not expect to find any mineral deposits. Up to some fifty kilometres inland, in an area called the coastal plains, the countryside was hilly with lots of palm trees and light forests. The elevation increased relative to the distance from the coast. Here were the coffee and the rubber plantations and some settlements. No unusual rocks were reported and we did not expect to find any mineral deposits. (A year later, Theo discovered a lower grade iron-ore deposit along the Mano River, this was brought into production some ten years later.)

Further inland, the country changed to a rougher terrain with many mountain ridges exposed in a general direction of south-west to north-east, controlling the river flows. It was heavily forested with deciduous trees of all sizes and heavy underbrush laced with huge vines. This part of the country was shown on the map as a blank area; it was our concession, north of Bomi Hills.

To make the exploration more effective, we intended to use Bomi Hills as our base camp, eliminating the six-days travel to and from

Monrovia. We needed the backing up of superintendent Beuken to use his organization for our supplies, mail and money as extension to Monrovia. When we discussed this with him, he gave us his full support. He had a good grasp of our situation as he had worked under similar circumstances with our general manager before. It turned out to be an effective support.

As some iron deposits had been reported east of Bomi Hills, near the villages Dobaton and Bambona, we intended to go there first. Afterwards we would continue to the north-east.

On the first day of this expedition, Theo and I woke up very early. By daybreak everybody was standing around the packed supplies. Some of our carriers were arguing with our overseer and refusing to take their loads. The arguments were about the weight differences between the boxes. They became louder and louder and went on and on. At last we got impatient and settled the problem. But by doing this, we undercut our overseer, who became reluctant to insist on his judgment. It took us an hour and a half to straighten out the situation before we could be on our way. This turned out to be only a small setback.

Two hours later, we reached a river. The ferry, that took us across, was a sleek canoe—a hollowed-out tree trunk—surprisingly stable and able to take four or five men plus their loads.

When everyone had crossed, we discovered we were short six men. That really upset us. They could have had an accident; they could be lost; or they could even have run away. We did not know our crew well enough to be sure. Fortunately, the trunk with the money was with our gang. Theo, our overseer and two headmen went immediately to look for the lost men, while I went ahead to the next village with the crew to wait. At the village, about an hour and a half later, the six missing men emerged from the bush from the opposite direction, carrying our beds, the cooking utensils and our office trunk. Theo and his men were not with them. I sent a runner after the search party and I anticipated it would take some time to find them. We were only two and a half hours away from our base camp at Bomi Hills. It made more sense to go back there and start over again the next day. But to me, it did not look good to come back and I decided to set up camp in this little village.

One of the men from the lost group came to me quite upset. While following us earlier, they had come to a split in the road and apparently had taken the wrong fork. They had walked half an hour in that direction and had come to a river. The headman had borrowed fifty cents from this man for the ferry crossing, which was all his savings and represented a week's earnings. Now he wanted his money back. I asked the headman why *he* had not told me this problem, since *he* was responsible for his men. The headman was uninterested in the money, caring only that he had got the men back to us. The upset man repeated that he paid for that crossing and now he wanted his money back. I agreed with him, told him that he would be paid and then laughed about this strange situation. The whole crew, who had crowded around us, started to laugh as well and the situation was defused. An hour later, Theo and the search party arrived in the village.

That afternoon we were able to watch the activities. Mid-afternoon the women started to prepare for their daily cooking of the rice. It was a social affair. Families sent for water, which was drawn from the river. Women, with sizeable, home-made, wooden buckets, walked leisurely to the river, chatting. They filled their buckets to the top and helped each other lift the heavy loads onto their heads. Balancing the buckets, without touching them, young and old walked back to their huts, along a rocky path. The youngest children were already carrying their buckets in perfect balance. My steward also went for water and returned, carrying the bucket on his head. While watching this, I remembered the children in Monrovia walking to school with their notebooks and bibles on their heads, leaving their hands free.

That night, after dinner, the children surrounded Theo and me. We figured we could entertain the crowd. We asked James, our steward, to place a tablecloth over the bridge table and set the kerosene lamp in the middle. Theo sat on one side and I sat on the other. Then we put our hands on the tablecloth and displaying a magnet in one hand. From their reactions I could tell that the children had never seen a magnet. We asked James to bring a razor-blade and placed it on the table. We took the magnet, hidden in one hand under the tablecloth where nobody could see it, and told the children to watch closely. Suddenly the razor-blade moved from one end of the table to the other. The children shrieked in utter amazement. After performing for some time, I tried to explain what we were doing. I was sure the children still did not understand what happened, but we received respect from the village crowd.

Before leaving the next morning, we paid for our stay. The exchange was in the form of barter. Compensation was made with tobacco leaves or salt—which were not locally available and which Jordense had added to our supplies—because here money did not exist as a medium of exchange. We established the payment of one tobacco leaf (the equivalent of three cents) per person, per night. Later on, I made it a practice of paying the town chief in full view of the population and at the end, the town chief got his *dash.* Everyone knew what to expect to receive and I did not interfere with the internal organization. At that time, I did not know it was common for travellers to stay in a town and use the hospitality of the townspeople without compensating. After hearing this, I made sure that when travelling through the countryside, the townspeople would be told by my crew, "White man always pay!"

On the trail that morning, Jimmy, the cook, wanted to buy some chickens at a three-hut settlement. A young woman appeared from one of the huts, wearing only a few strings of beads. She asked forty cents for each chicken. After bartering, Jimmy bought them for twenty-five cents each. What the woman could do with the money was anybody's guess. Nobody seemed to notice what, to me, looked like a provocative situation: the almost naked, voluptuous woman, with a chicken in her hands and the well dressed Jimmy, bartering.

I had been watching Jimmy, as I had had a say in his hiring. I had told him earlier, that if he was a good worker and a competent cook, he could stay with me after the expedition. I also paid his asking salary of five dollars per month because he claimed to be a full-fledged cook, having trained in the French embassy.

We had ferried across one river the day before, but there were still two big creeks to go. These creeks had been bridged by cutting a tall tree in such a way so that the tree fell across the creek. After trimming the branches, these trees became narrow footbridges. It was amazing to watch our carriers surefootedly crossing these bridges, with their loads balanced on their heads, keeping in step with the springing up and down of the tree. I felt unsure about my own ability to keep my balance and get across. I was afraid I would fall off and be badly hurt in the branches or on the rocks below. "No problem," said my steward. "I'll carry you across, just sit on my back and close your eyes." I hesitated. But it seemed worthwhile trying and very likely safer, then crossing on my own, so I accepted the invitation. He carried me across without a problem and before I realized it, I was on the other side.

When we arrived in the next village, Dobaton, which had perhaps thirty huts, the crew was already there. The town chief provided a two-room hut for our party. Our steward set up our two field cots in one room. The supply boxes were deposited in the other room. The cook and steward slept on top of the boxes and four other men slept in the same room on mats on the floor. The rest of our carriers were quartered in other huts. The family that lived in our hut had been moved in with others.

That afternoon, Jimmy started to prepare our meal, while we relaxed. I was watching him catch a chicken for dinner when I noticed that all three chickens had broken legs. I realized that when he bought the chickens from the woman that morning, Jimmy had tied the legs together and with a stick between the legs of the chickens, balanced the load over his shoulder. I remembered thinking that was a smart way to carry the chickens. However, when I realized how these chickens were hanging uncomfortably with their heads down and their legs broken by the stick, I told Jimmy that it was cruel and he must find another solution. He said that was unnecessary, because in a few days these chickens would be eaten. That night after dinner I asked Jimmy to make some cages. Reluctantly he made them, muttering, "What a waste of time!" From that day on, chickens travelled in cages, hanging from a stick carried over Jimmy's shoulder.

Theo and I walked to the creek for our bath. The whole town was there. The women and children took off, whatever minimal clothing they had on before bathing. A short distance downstream the men stripped, covering their genitals with one hand. We went quite some distance downstream, out of sight, to take our bath.

The following day we did our first real exploration work, investigating a known iron outcrop. At daybreak we issued cutlasses and axes to our carriers, who now became our clearing crew. Theo and I took our instruments. Our guides were the town chief and all the local elite—some thirty men—who assisted in showing their local iron deposit. They hoped that if they showed valuable information, they would get a hefty dash; whoever was present could expect to be included in it.

It was, of course, impossible to do a proper prospecting job while hampered by the locals, but we didn't want to be impolite. We decided to get rid of our unwanted associates as quickly and subtly as possible. We arrived at the overgrown outcrop after about an hour's walking. There we had part of our crew cut a trail along the outcrop, while the rest of the crew made a grid, cutting trails perpendicular to the first trail every one hundred metres in both directions. As the outcrop of the deposit was harder than the surrounding formation, it created a high, sloping hill above the countryside with—at the high point—quite a steep cliff. We invited our following to join us in walking these perpendicular trails. From way down, we climbed up the hill and descended on the other side, where we waited until everybody arrived and then crossed over to the next trail and repeated this climb, crossing over the outcrop, again and again. During these climbs there was a lot of palaver about rocks and I heard that bomi meant "heavy rock" in the local language. The heat increased by the hour and everybody perspired.

Each crossing took about an hour and we expected that this would not be very interesting for these people. After the first hour, boredom set in and our party shrunk to about half its size. Three hours later, we were on our own. We were wet and tired, but we started taking proper measurements, magnetometer readings and samples, and making notes. It was quite late when we returned to the village. When we arrived, we made sure that the town chief got his dash. We were dead-tired, so had our dinner, a short evening and retired early.

That night I tossed around and had a hard time getting to sleep, because Theo, a sound sleeper, was snoring loudly. For several nights, I had asked him to keep his mouth closed. He did so readily, but after a little while he started snoring again. This night I asked him again to stop snoring, but five minutes later the noise was back. I knew there must be a better way to stop the snoring, so I got up and in a corner of the hut I found one of his socks from that day, smelly and wet from sweat. When the snoring started again, I lifted the mosquito netting and put the sock into his mouth. I left the hut quickly and waited until the cursing stopped and he settled down to sleep again, which took quite some time. It was worth it, because Theo never snored again. (Later, when his wife Cor asked how I had got her husband to stop snoring, I left it up to Theo to tell her.)

We continued our investigation of the deposit and completed it in two more days. The last night we sat down and discussed the results of the exploration. We were able to estimate the tonnage of the deposit and came to the conclusion that this deposit of a few million tons made little economic sense. Later on, I learned that thirty-five years later the deposit was mined, once the truck road was extended.

On the seventh day of the expedition we moved east to check on other known iron deposits inside the concession. That night we camped in the bush. It was a beautiful evening. Theo and I were reading outside the tent, relaxing, without realizing that ants were invading the tent. When we were ready to go to bed, the ants were all over our belongings. They came from all directions. We called our steward and cook, who put big fires around the tent. We used six spray cans of D.D.T. inside the tent. After an hour and a half we had the attack under control. The next morning there were still ants, half-dead with spasms, suffering from D.D.T. exposure. They were hard to kill.

The next day we moved on and by late that afternoon we reached Bambona, a sizeable town and the home of a paramount chief. It was known that the countryside held three iron deposits. We stayed in Bambona a week and of course we introduced ourselves to both the paramount chief and the town chief.

We decided to let Beuken know where we were. He could forward our progress report to head office and send our mail. A dispatcher was designated and he returned on the third day. Although it took us three days to travel to and from Bomi Hills, this man had walked it in one day. For Theo, it was nice to hear from Cor, his wife, about his son and for me, a letter, in which both my parents wrote the news, was a moral booster. We instituted this dispatch service on a weekly basis.

With one of the small outcrops, we tried to complete the investigation in one day. On our way to town, late in the afternoon, we had to stop at a creek to locate a spot where we could cross. This was a pleasant opportunity for our crew to take a bath. Theo and I were enjoying the fun they had. I stood facing the creek,not realizing that I was on top of two parallel highways of ants, until one ant had reached my neck. I located one on my hand, then I realized they were crawling all over me and eventually biting me under my shirt. One even reached my crotch. It happened that an uncle of mine had joined the British army in Singapore after the war. Before my departure to Liberia he had given me his Gurkha uniform, complete with puttees, and that was what I wore. Because of these puttees I did not feel the ants crawling on my pants. There were ten men around me picking off the ants, where I felt them biting, but there was only one way to get control and that was to take off all my clothes so that they could see the ants on my white body. By that time it was dark. In agony I first unwound my puttees before I could take off my trousers. After stripping, my crew made my underpants and shoes ant-free, so that I could use these. They bundled all my clothes on a long stick and we walked home in the dark. Our cook wondered why we had not returned before dark. He took the kerosene lamp and, together with the town chief and some bystanders, went looking for us. We met them half-way. Quite late that night I walked into town in my undershorts and of course all the townspeople were watching and laughing at the white man. I never wore puttees again.

On the second night the paramount chief and the town chief came to visit Theo and me in our tent after dinner. It was not easy to keep a conversation going, as we had no idea what their interests were. I had a battery-operated radio, so we turned on some music. That was fascinating for our visitors, who had never seen or heard a radio. It was very likely that they had never travelled outside their district. After a while, they got bored with our type of music, so I offered them a cigar from my cigar box. The paramount chief grabbed in the box with both hands and took hold of some eight cigars, which he put in his robe pockets. When the box was passed on to the town chief, he did the same. I was quite sure they would not smoke these wonderful cigars, but chew on them. However, I could not say anything about it and after some time they left.

The next evening they arrived again for more "conversation" but we had had enough. They thought they had a good thing going: entertainment and cigars. Again we turned on the radio and I told them if they wanted to listen to the music, they should not talk. Then I offered them cigarettes, but this time I held the package and let only one cigarette slip out. I could see the disappointment on their faces and our guests soon left.

After a week in this town we moved on to the north-east, prospecting on the way. We stopped first in Bambuta.

The trail between Bambona and Bambuta had been a perfect road, cleared and levelled all the way. It was an abandoned truck road with only two curves, though it was a five-hour walk. The terrain was favourable for road building. The clan must have built it some five years before. Very likely the chiefs had convinced the clan of the importance of having a full-fledged truck road with proper ditches. The connection to the main road, fifty kilometres away, was missing and this made the road useless. The forest was slowly taking possesion of it again, trees and brushes sprouted all over, ant hills were built and the footpath wound around these. The wet season had washed away the soft parts of the road and re-routed the ditches. The road deteriorated; all efforts had been in vain.

Later on I met a clan building a road. The work was done democratically. The chief had everybody in town go to the construction site, where he would sit on a stool or chair and point out who would do what chore: cut trees; clear brush; move obstacles or boulders; fill baskets with dirt taken from the high spots and dumped in the low spots. Usually the women and children would go along, very likely to fetch water and to cook. I was surprised to see how well this system worked out, although it could still take years to complete the road.

Cleared truck road in the middle of nowhere

In Bambuta we met the clan chief, who was travelling in the area. When he heard that two strangers were in town, he decided to make a detour to meet us. Theo and I talked with him in the town centre in front of the palaver house, our overseer acting as interpreter. Everybody was listening and interested in what was being discussed. After a while, I offered the clan chief a cigarette from my package. As there were one and a half cigarettes sticking out, he took them both. The package was passed on to the town chief, who also took two cigarettes. I looked at Theo and we laughed and I thought: here we go again.

Two days later we reached Boporo, a district town, where we took accomodation. After dinner we visited the district commissioner in his compound. As Theo and I walked into the compound, we were surprized by the size of the layout, it looked bigger than the town itself. The compound had been levelled and at the far end were three huge government buildings, neatly lined up and flanked by two sizeable huts. All buildings were white-washed mud huts. The centre building was the palaver house, which could easily hold a hundred people. On the right were the large barracks for the forty soldiers and beside that was the jail. On the other side were government offices, as well as the home of the district commissioner and beside that, the private palaver house for him and his family. It was there that we were received. To me, this set-up far outweighed the importance of this district. Building this compound must have been a real burden for the tribe.

That night there was a full moon. It was so bright that I could see my shadow, almost like midday. We were told there would be a dance. In the bigger towns there were always drummers of all ages from about seven years and up. The drum beat was created by the tapping of fingers; no drumsticks were used. Each drum had its distinctive sound. These drums were hollow tree sections, either closed or solid at one end with a skin tightened over the other end. That night the dance started slowly but when there was enough enthusiasm, the tempo increased. The drummers also used calabashes, a type of gourd, in which they put pebbles. The movements of the calabashes were syncopated and I could feel the rhythm of a rhumba. The drummers accompanied the song, made up by one of the dancers. The soloist began with a six-note refrain introduction of: "Ho..., ho..., ho..., ho..., ho..., ho...," and then sang his story, followed by a different refrain by the dancers: "Ha-haah..., ha-haah...". Then the soloist interrupted with his own refrain: "Ho..., ho..., ho..., ho..., ho..., ho...," continuing the story and the melody.

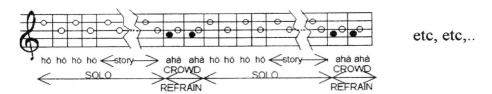

etc, etc,..

The overseer told us that these stories could be about the happenings of that day; about the food, the town, family and friends of the tribe, or about the funny way this white man travelled. At fitst I thought it sounded dreary, but eventually I could appreciate a good rhythm.

The dancers walked close behind each other and formed a circle: first five men, then four women, then some children, then again a bunch of men, women and children, old and young, dancing close behind each other, almost touching....always closing the circle. The circle of the thirty-odd people was big enough to allow a person who felt like dancing a solo to jump into the centre and perform, while the other dancers watched. The dancers moved on the rhythm of the drum through their knees, taking small steps. The rotating circle moved slowly through town. If there was enough participation, a second circle was formed. The dancers seemed to get high on this rhythm. The circle favoured our presence; I thought they hoped for a dash. They stopped and took a local drink, cane juice, but soon started up again, "Ho..., ho..., ho..., ho..., ho..., ho...," and the drummers joined in. The circle was in motion again, rotating and moving.

Once in a refrain I heard, "One dollar fifty." I found out from our headman that the song was about the soloist, who had invited any woman to join him for this amount, but nobody accepted the offer and he was sad. This dancing went on all night until early in the morning, without stopping. But at daybreak everybody was present for work.

On leaving town, we noticed that the district commissioner had started to build a truck road with forced labour. We passed two prisoners working on it, guarded by two soldiers. They were required to dig, fill baskets with dirt and dump the contents of these baskets at the low part of the road, under the supervision of these soldiers with rifles. There was a guard at either end of the work area. The prisoners needed their hands and feet free. Along their back a stick was tied at their waist and their neck. This pole stuck an arm's length above their head. If anyone tried to run away, the pole would get caught in the underbrush and tree branches. This was an easy and simple method to prevent them from running away.

We continued to the north-east. It was the end of March and the wind had shifted to the north. The nights were very cold. According to our overseer, the wind originated in the Sahara. We were glad that Jordense had provided us with two blankets each, we needed them. Our crew did not suffer because they were quartered with the locals, who kept fires going inside their huts. Sometimes the men found it too cold to work early in the morning and they took a fire along in the cooking pot to the workplace, claiming that this would get rid of the cold. Of course, it would get warmer and warmer during the day, until by noon the heat was almost unbearable.

Two days later we were camping in a village. The tent was set up and our crew had accommodations in the town huts. The bridge table was unfolded and we had our chairs brought out, ready for a quiet afternoon. Suddenly, our steward, James, came running to us very agitated and yelling, "The go go row, boh, the go go row!" We did not understand what this was all about, but after calming him down, we found out what had happened. He discovered a goat had entered the tent, found the bananas inside and eaten them all. So he meant to say, "The goat goes around, boss." We laughed.

We also realized that there was a problem. Who was going to pay for these bananas? Our steward thought that the owner of the goat should pay for this meal, but the owner was away at the time. We thought it better to tell James that it was our job to keep the tent closed and he should forget about the lost bananas.

After four weeks of work without a break, our supplies were low and we decided to return to Bomi Hills. This expedition had taught us a lot about our concession and the type of prospecting we could expect. We had travelled trails that were seldom straight and with limited vision. Usually I could not see farther than three carriers in front of me. It was said that these were elephant trails. I never once saw an elephant, but was told that there were still some in the eastern province. Our overseer told us that according to custom, the trails had to be kept in passable condition, and this was the responsibility of the towns at either end. Who controlled that? It was not important to these people. We crawled over fallen trees and moved around rocks on these trails. If we wanted to go to a specific outcrop, we had to cut our own trail. We got some inkling about the local settlements, which ranged from a few huts to the odd little village thirty to fifty kilometres apart, and about the population and its customs.

This expedition had started with some blunders, but we were able to make the necessary corrections. We had visited a number of iron deposits, met some chiefs and got to know our crew. We had learned to delegate the running of the expedition to our overseer so that Theo and I could concentrate on geology and prospecting. It was time to start working on our own.

We arrived in Bomi Hills a week later and paid off the crew.

The Second Expedition: Beginner's Luck

From now on the party was over. Theo and I were going in different directions. We felt confident in our work and we did not have to double up anymore. All my life I had wished to be my own boss. This time it was not *we,* but *me* going on expedition. We decided that if one of us had something promising turn up, the other could take a second look at it, if necessary. Theo would go to the north-west and I to the north-east. Both areas were expected to have sizeable alluvial gold deposits. I wondered where I would possibly find a profitable deposit. There must be one out there.

We had to divide the crew and split the tools. The overseer, one headman with his gang and the steward, James, went with Theo. He had to look for another cook and hunter. The others went with me. I made our headman and hunter, Daniel, the temporary overseer. Also, I was going to see if John, the helper of our overseer, would work out as a steward for me. It was a reasonable division. My crew was sixteen men. We split the tools and I got the tent. We ordered lamps, kitchen pots and pans, and another office trunk. When these arrived from Monrovia, I was ready to go.

It was one month before the rainy season. Liberia has two distinct seasons: the dry season from December to April and the wet season from May to November. The average temperature year-round was 25 to 28 degrees Celcius with high humidity. Because the mornings were cooler, I started the expedition at daybreak. By mid-morning the sweat was already soaking my clothes.

Travelling north, I tested the creeks for heavy minerals, took rock samples of the ridges, noted the strikes. For the distances I used a hand counter, clicking every fourth step—about three metres— and registering the direction with the compass. At night I made rudimentary maps.

A week later I stopped in a village of approximately twenty huts. During the night, some one had stolen rice from one of the villagers. At daybreak there were many palavers. As strangers, we were suspected,

31

but eventually the culprit was caught. It was fortunate that he was not one of my crew. The town chief called all the people including my party to the town square. There were about sixty in total and all had to attend the punishment: twenty lashes with a bamboo reed, applied by the victim. The culprit was tied over a fallen tree, his pants were pulled down, the victim was given the reed and he executed the punishment, while the town chief counted. The victim delivered the first strokes slowly and deliberately as hard as he could, but then he got more and more agitated and the tempo increased. From the fifteenth stroke on, I did not think the culprit was really hurt. The only risk for him was, it could damage his kidneys, if the beating was not on his bottom, but higher on the back. The execution of local law was direct and a deterrent to all the onlookers.

Because of this theft and the palavers that followed between the townspeople and my crew, I lost a day's work. This annoyed me.

Still we moved on and in late afternoon John, my steward-designate, and I walked on a trail which came to a split. One trail was used more than the other. There we met a local hunter and I asked, pointing to the used trail, "What is the name of the next town?"

"Yes!" the hunter said

"What is the town's name?" Changing the sentence because I was not sure that he understood me.

"No!" he said.

"List - en - good, — what - is - the - name - of - the - town?" I repeated slowly, pointing to the trail.

"Yes!"

I felt helpless and looked at John, who turned to the hunter, saying:

"Wah, tou, naa." and he got the right answer.

After a few days I noticed that, because of the interruption of the rice theft, the crew and I were rested. We performed better and did more the following week. I realized then that I had to re-evaluate our work pattern. Before we started on our expeditions, Jordense had not brought up the work standards and we had not asked. In Europe the standard was still forty-eight hours a week, while in the U.S. it was forty hours a week. We had stuck to eight hours a day during our expeditions, without a break. Our men had no notion of labour relations or of work times and they did not complain. From that moment on, I made the rule that, wherever we were, we did not work on a Sunday.

Relaxing in an abandoned sugar cane factory on a Sunday

By law, Saturdays were paydays and after making the payouts, I kept my money box open for whoever wanted to deposit his money for safe keeping. Usually the workmen would hang on to some change for little purchases and ask me to keep the balance to be paid out at the base camp upon our return.

This served both sides well, because the following week I used the same money to meet the payroll, as long as I made sure that on my return to the base camp there was enough money to meet the final payment to each worker. This was my banking operation and it considerably reduced the weight and risk of carrying a fair amount of money relatively unprotected. On our first expedition of more than a month we had started out with over a thousand dollars in copper, nickel and silver coins. I was able to reduce this to only forty or fifty dollars per expedition, as long as I made sure the savings were readily available in Bomi Hills.

I officially made John my steward. I had noticed that our first overseer had selected the best man for himself to do all his chores and to carry his trunk. Our present overseer had John as his helper. But since our overseer was gone with Theo, John became available and to me he looked like a good candidate for the job of steward. John was from the Bussy tribe, about twenty-five years old and quite a bit taller than the other carriers. He was healthy, strong, trustworthy, intelligent, handy and a very happy fellow. Through Jimmy, our French-trained cook, John's training got the finishing touch, almost like a butler. He was in charge of the household money and at the evening meal gave account of the purchases. He repaired clothing, ironed after washing. Before an expedition he packed my trunk. And once a month he had to cut my hair, something he hated to do. I thought that perhaps he did not like to touch my head because of tribal custom. After six months John was always dressed in

white and even bought himself a white helmet. Then one day he served
at dinner with a towel over his left forearm, the final French touch.

I travelled to the north-east area and found many tributaries, some
likely with gold. I met a local prospector and as we walked toward his
workings, he asked how I analyzed a deposit like this. It looked like a
haphazard operation with trees fallen criss-crossed in all directions and
pits dug here and there. The prospector invited me to check out the deposit but I did not think he expected me to wash for gold and neither did
my crew. For knowing how to do this I could only thank my former
professor of economic geology for his thoughtfulness. When I had got
the job in Liberia, he had called me to his office and said, "You'd better
know how to pan for gold." He opened a drawer in his desk, took out a
vial with gold dust, sprinkled some gold flakes on a piece of paper, shoved
twenty flakes to the side, led me to the lab where he had a tub filled with
sand, and dumped in the twenty flakes. He told the laboratory employee
to stir this thoroughly. Before leaving, he looked at me and said, "Now
Sir, come back to see me when you can manage to wash out of the tub all
twenty flakes at one time." The next day I started to pan with a flat,
shallow tub that had a cone-shaped bottom. At the end of the afternoon I
had not recovered one flake. But after a week I was able to recover the
flakes quite easily.

Panning for gold in a tributary

Now I confidently took a pan, jumped in the creek, went to where the overburden had been removed, filled it with gravel and washed the pan. To everybody's surprise, as well as mine, there was a nugget the size of my fingertip in the pan as well as some gold dust. I said, "Beginner's luck." This was the first time that I panned for gold in Liberia and the last time I panned a nugget. I was interested to know what the value of this nugget was. I did not have a scale and the only way was to improvise. I knew that the American money was based on coins that were in relation to their weights. One dollar weighed forty grams and the weight of ten dimes equaled four quarters, which equaled one dollar. The weight of the nugget was almost twelve grams or a quarter of a Troy ounce.

I stayed in the camp a few days, trying to discover the source of the deposit. Walking up the creek, I came upon a ridge with a quartz vein. I chipped off a piece of the vein and with my magnifier saw gold-coloured mineral glistening. I thought, "This is gold!" Was I ever excited. I did not tell anyone about it. It can't be true, finding gold in your first quartz vein. That night I read up on this type of outcrop in my geology book and it warned to be careful not to confuse gold with pyrite, also known as fool's gold. The next day I went back to the same spot and looked again for the gold glistening, but now it was brown, having oxidized and I knew that gold does not oxidize. I had almost made a fool of myself.

After evaluating his concession for three days, I told the prospector what I figured he made out of these workings; he was surprised at how close my estimate was. A week later I passed through this camp again. This man impressed me so much that I offered him the job of prospector and overseer at a rate of about three times the amount of money he made in his creek. He accepted. That was a real nugget.

Travelling together, I heard the story of the prospector's life bit by bit. His full name was Elisia Howard Dean and he had been baptized in the Lutheran mission in Zorzor. He must have been in his late twenties. His people, from the Bussy tribe in the northern part of the country, considered him to be an educated man, having been instructed to the sixth grade level at that mission. He had worked in a gold creek for some time and become a prospector. He could efficiently wash for gold and he never missed the opportunity to look for diamonds, which he spotted two years later. Dean became a top overseer. For two years we travelled together through Liberia. He moved his family to the Bomi village. One day he asked me if his brother, introduced as "same father and different mother," could work for us. In my time his half-brother became a headman. I learned that Dean's father had been a paramount chief in the Bussy tribe, in Zorzor. When we travelled with sixty or more carriers, Dean was in charge and the expedition ran without friction. I noticed that he had a natural authority and he was firm, but fair, with his people. Later when we travelled through the Bussy country in the north, he introduced me to his mother. With all the experiences that we shared, Dean and I became friends. I think he worked for the Liberia Mining Company for a long time after I left. I have always wondered what became of him, as, at that time, he was sure he would return to his tribe.

Once again we were low in supplies and it was time to return to Bomi Hills. On the way home I thought about the good things that had happened: an A-1 prospector as overseer, a steward and even a real gold nugget.

It was a gratifying expedition. But still the economic deposit evaded me. Would my next expedition be more fortunate?

The Third Expedition:
Unexpected Encounters

The night before every expedition I wondered if *this* would be the "time of discovery." There were leads, but they seemed to fizzle out. The work was tedious. However, there were always unexpected developments that made expeditions lively.

Expeditions were beginning to be routine. This time Dean took care of running the expedition.

Start of an expedition, in front of the laboratory, Bomi Hills
The hotel is behind the laboratory. In the left background is my hut

Dean and John were busy getting the loads ready early. I would sleep until John knocked on the army cot saying, "Boss, daybreak boss!" I would answer, "All right John," and lift up the mosquito netting, put my feet into slippers, get up and look for the water bucket with soap, facecloth, comb, shaving material, mirror, toothbrush and the towel hanging close by. Sometimes the waterbucket was in the middle of town on a low bench or on an overturned, hip-high rice mortar beside the tent and sometimes on the ground. In the meantime, all the loads were checked for weight and lined up. My breakfast of bread, fried egg, jam and tea was ready and by the time I finished, my cot was packed and everything was ready to go. Before leaving, I visited the chief, in order to find out about the promised carriers. Usually there was a discussion about how far they would go and their pay. After that was settled, we dashed those who had quartered our crew.

"Let's go!" was the sign that every man could take up his load. Most carriers wove themselves a thick ring of straw or cloth and placed this on their head as a cushion, before getting the load on top of it.

John was always in a good mood, singing, "Let's go! Let's go!" while he gave everybody a hand placing the loads on their heads. I found it fascinating to see this column of carriers leaving town with Jimmy, the cook, in between them carrying only two lanterns. When all the men were on their way, I would say my thanks to the chief, give him his dash and leave. Dean would close the ranks to make sure that nobody was left behind. John would carry the sample bags, my water bottle, raincoat if required and a cutlass for clearing the underbrush or making a path. I would carry my magnifier on a chain around my neck. In the pouch I had a notebook, pencils, compass, magnetometer, tape and counter; in my belt was my geological hammer. Soon we would catch up with the crew.

The crew would spread itself out, each man walking at his own speed. After the first hour I passed here and there a carrier's load lying beside the trail. The men would go into the bush and a little time later they would reappear, relieved. Mid-morning we would stop and wait for the last man to catch up before continuing.

If we came to an untested creek a test pit was dug. One of the men would wash the gravel and the heavy minerals were put in a vial and labelled.

Upon reaching our destination, Jimmy would start a fire, if possible with two trees side by side. He had some moss and two quartz stones in a small box and could make a fire in no time, even in the rainy season. By knocking a spark and blowing on the moss, he soon had a fire roaring, the water boiling and within half an hour John would call, "Bath ready!" Then I had a hot bath in the tub. Afterwards I got dressed in dry clothing before dinner. The crew took their bath in the creek, together with the townspeople.

Dean issued food: rice, palm oil, salt and meat if we had it. His responsibility also was to acquired the rice locally, whenever we needed to replenish our stock. The meat depended on what our hunter shot that day or the day before. One of our carriers was promoted to hunter, which was an honour and an easy job, as he did not carry a load. He received the shotgun and one cartridge. He got only one cartridge to reduce shooting for speculation, to make sure the animal would be killed and not simply wounded and left to die in agony. If he came back empty-handed, with or without a used cartridge, he was considered to be a poor hunter, demoted and another man became the hunter.

Our carriers ate mostly monkey meat and the odd antelope. Relatively small pieces were issued, the balance was smoked and kept for the following days.

We took along cast-iron cooking pots for the crew. Four or five men would combine their cooking. They gathered dead wood for a fire and went to the cook for some embers. Then they fetched water, cleaned the rice if necessary and smoked the meat. One of them would talk to the townspeople or go into the bush for their "small little something," which was green leaves, pepper, fish, worms, snails, frogs, ants, honey, vegetables, bananas, lime— whatever they could find to make the meal more palatable.

Smoked monkey meat carried in gold washing pans

After the food issue, Dean had a first aid session, dispensing liniment for sore backs or disinfectant for cuts in the soles of feet. John would serve a cup of coffee in grand style in a mug on a tray. Then he brought a bridge table and a lamp. Dinner was served: chicken soup, rice with chicken, some vegetables, then a cup of hot chocolate.

After dinner John, Jimmy and Dean ate together in the kitchen using the leftovers of my meal. They ate everything right down to the chicken bones. Their teeth were perfect and strong from not being exposed to sugar.

The evenings were usually a quiet affair, spent drawing a map, working out notes of the day, reading and once a week writing home. The crew talked with the townspeople. This became our routine.

The unexpected shock came three days later. I noticed that I seemed to have worms again. On the way home from the last expedition I had contracted tapeworm. It was horrible. However, my father, a doctor, sent me medicines from Holland to get rid of the problem. This time I was upset and considered a return to our base camp to contact the doctor in Monrovia. I had instructed Jimmy and John to be extremely careful and to thoroughly cook all vegetables and meat. In the Interior my toilet was usually a hole, with two sticks pressed into the ground on each side of it. These sticks were forked on the top, and in the hollow of the two sticks was a horizontal stick. I could sit on this "john." After every use, lime was dumped into the hole as disinfectant. This time, when I used the "john" and completed my business, I noticed lots of white worms moving around. To make sure that I could describe the problem exactly to the doctor, I watched my next bowel movement closely and I could not believe what I saw. The moment I relieved myself, huge flies were buzzing around and within the first second the flies deposited little larvae. The next time I was more alert and I counted that the first fly deposited twenty-one larvae. I could not have imagined it was possible, if I had not seen it myself. This observation solved my worm problem.

Continuing to prospect, we ended up in a town late on a Saturday, It was payday. Sunday was our day off, so I tried to sleep a little longer. Mid-morning John came into the tent and said that I had better get up because there was a crowd outside with a surprise! Reluctantly I arose and when I came out of the tent, I could not believe what I saw. Standing in front of the tent was a man with a light blue, thigh-thick, three to four-metre long snake. I did not know what kind it was and never found out. The snake was crawling out of his hand with its head in front of the man, but very close to me. The man was pulling the snake towards him at the same speed as the snake was crawling towards me. There must have been some sixty people watching this to see my reaction. I stood still and did not move. Suddenly I realized this was a performance. After fifteen minutes, I asked the man to pull in the snake and then I gave him a dash of cigarettes, tobacco leaves and two dimes. This kind of generous dash expressed more my shock than my appreciation. Then I asked John for my tea, sat down, and enjoyed my Sunday.

We continued prospecting in this valley and a few days later the crew stopped in the middle of the day. One of the men said, "Honey!" From that moment on there was no way I could convince the crew that we had a schedule to meet. They all came together, put down their loads and looked up at the sky. I did not see anything, but they got the axes ready and started to chop at the trunk of a very tall tree. The men were all agitated and working really hard. I let them go ahead. We had been more than a month in the bush and this was quite boring for the carriers. This was their distraction.

After a good hour, the tree slowly leaned over and then, with a huge crash, it fell. In the meantime, others had made a fire. With an axe the fallen tree was sounded and at the edge of the hollow sound on both ends, holes were cut. When these holes were big enough, burning leaves were pushed into one end. The leaves made a lot of smoke. Out of the other end the bees scrambled. When no more bees escaped, the men chopped open the section between the two holes and scooped honey into buckets. After two hours, they had two full buckets.

When I looked up, I could still see the bees flying around and around at their original entry spot, trying to locate their hive. I resigned myself to watching their smart organization. It was quite late when we arrived in the new camp, but nobody complained. The crew shared the honey with the camp people. My reward was honey on my bread the next morning.

In the Interior, with so few settlements and virtually no traffic, it seemed a rarity for the natives to see a white man. That evening, while I was sitting in front of my tent after dinner, John came and said that a woman had come, who had never seen a white man. That woman could have walked two or three days to see the white man. "Could she touch your skin to see if it is real?" I was not busy and I shook her hand and John gave her a tobacco leaf, a treat in the Interior.

We continued north and the next Sunday, while I sat reading in front of the tent in the morning, I noticed a man coming out of his hut, looking around furtively. Suddenly he reached for the straw covering of his roof and took out a bundle of iron money and then he walked away. He never realized that I was watching him.

An iron cent was a staff about forty centimetres long, a little less than half a centimetre thick, twisted in the middle like a bad screw. One end was flattened to the size of a dollar; this was called the ear. The other end had a three-centimetre perpendicular strip, called the foot. The people thought this iron cent had a soul. A local blacksmith had probably made these "coins." Because of its size, this currency was unwieldy and I never came across it in trading. I saw five- and ten-cent iron pieces, each one bigger than the previous one. This iron money suggested there could be iron deposits in the surrounding countryside.

But the local economy did not actually require money. The forest provided for all the people's needs. Food was available in fruit, fowl and fish, cassava and rice. The building material for walls was woven sticks sealed with mud and roofs were covered with palm leaves. For clothing, the natives used hide or woven straw.

To the local people, my expedition must have seemed like a kind of circus, the happening of a lifetime. Some twenty men falling suddenly into the midst of their quiet existence. A white man was a curiosity alone. The white man had all kinds of mysterious things around his neck and waist, spent time looking at rocks, hammering at these rocks and putting the rubble in bags. For what? The men setting up a tent. Each man performing tasks in an orderly manner, using all kind of gadgets, which they had not seen and never knew existed. Two or three days later these strange people were gone, never to return.

After four weeks of travel I had completed a segment of our concession and it was time to return to Bomi Hills. The signs for the start of the rainy season were there. The sky was overcast; on the odd day we had a heavy rain. Travelling would soon become difficult. We had to stop.

Bomi Hills during the Rainy Season

Our expeditions were discontinued for the time being. We wondered what this season would bring. It turned out to be quite different from what we expected.

During the rainy season, from May to November, the creeks swelled to rivers and flooded the countryside, creating huge swamps. The last week of our expedition I travelled in this rainy season. It was difficult, sometimes dangerous or impossible. I did not have any dry clothing and those clothes that were in my trunk got mouldy, along with my books. To counteract the mouldiness John had to iron all my clothing. On top of that, if one of us accidently touched the canvas, the tent would leak at that spot. Because of the constant evaporation in the tropical heat, I got colder and colder and my skin would shrivel. I never felt warm. Working in this drizzle was trying.

Theo returned from his expedition. He had discovered a tourmaline deposit, high in gold and he was all excited, but had to wait for better weather to establish the extent of the mineralization.

By now Theo and I had become used to the tropical weather, although the increased humidity made it uncomfortable. My attitude also had changed. I remembered that, in Holland, during the cold winter of 1944-45, when we had no fuel, I had made up my mind to never again complain about the heat. So I convinced myself that it was only "nice and warm" and that seemed to make the heat more bearable. Of course it was psychological.

Theo and I expected to assist in the development of the mine where necessary, but we discovered that the planning of the mining operations, along with the production targets and equipment selections, was the responsibility of our manager and his assistant. This was our time to relax. We started to work out the data we had collected. Our crews were incorporated in the work of superintendent Beuken and they ended up clearing the outcrop.

Our Bomi Hills community increased from three to four staff members with the arrival of the surveyor Hubert Viola, who was about our age. He had moved in with us on the spare cot and we got along well. He had his own survey crew and was working on a topographical map of the mine site and the location of the incoming railroad track. Hubert was Polish and had been enlisted by the Germans during the war and stationed on the coast in Holland. As a dispatcher on a motorcycle he was able to assist the Dutch Underground, through which he got to know a Dutch girl named Dora. After the war, he stayed in Holland, married his sweetheart and they now had a son the same age as Theo's. Dora was to arrive three months later. The construction on Hubert's bungalow made good progress.

When it was time for Theo's wife, Cor, to arrive, Theo went to Monrovia to meet her. The wives of our company employees arrived by boat and had to disembark onto barges in open sea. For Cor, who carried her child in her arms, this was frightening. The weather was rough and the barges were rising and falling in the four-metre swell. Passengers had to anticipate the correct moment to step from the ship's ladder onto the barge. A sailor swept Cor and the child into his arms and carried them over. It was a harrowing experience. Theo and his family stayed a week in the company guest-house, shopping at the abundantly-stocked stores along the waterfront. When they returned, they moved into their bungalow and James became their steward.

The evenings in Bomi Hills were so relaxing. I usually heard the hiss of the crickets, which was penetrating and could go on for hours and hours. Close to the swamp, I could hear the frogs croaking, one calling, the other answering, and then the whole colony becoming involved. Usually John had bought some chickens and these were clucking around the hut. They were about one-third the size of the chickens in our country. Jimmy, the cook, did not feed these chickens; they had to get their own food, which was only worms and insects. That was very likely the reason that they tasted gamy. The eggs also had a stronger flavour. At night the chickens were not caged, but left loose. They settled on the roof of the hut, where the snakes could not get them. When we travelled in the bush, the chickens would settle on a branch above my tent. During my time in Liberia, I lost only one chicken, very likely to a snake.

This time I was not under pressure from the expedition to work on my notes at night and I had more time for the people around me. I had a chance to observe Jimmy and I realized how fortunate I was to get him as my cook. He had been employed in the French embassy and had learned French cuisine. He was always cleanly dressed and he had style, which I noticed in the manner how he trained John. As a cook, I paid him five dollars a month, which upset the other employees, because the going rate was between four and four-fifty a month. The most important job of a cook on an expedition was to be able to make a fire under *any* circumstances, even when it was raining. Jimmy had done well on this account. The next important thing for a cook was to make sure that all the sand was removed from the rice. We called it "the acid test." A small piece of sand in the rice on your plate was a horrible experience. When chewing, it felt like you were losing a tooth. When we had a small piece of sand on our plate, Jimmy was called. He had to see the rock and he knew, as a good cook, that it was *not* acceptable.

Because Jimmy prepared the meals, he also did the buying. For a man who had eaten rice all his life, Jimmy had developed a taste far superior than ours. He would go to the market, where there were, perhaps, eight bags of rice. To me they looked the same, but he tasted them all and decided, which type of rice *I* would like best. This could be compared to bread and Europeans, who could taste the differences between white bread, brown bread, whole-wheat bread, French bread or Italian bread. I found out that Jimmy could not taste that difference; for him all bread tasted the same, though he baked bread very well.

One morning I returned early from the laboratory. There was a woman coming with a bowl of about twenty eggs for sale. Jimmy was sitting outside in front of the kitchen. While the woman waited, he took each egg out of the bowl and held the round end of the egg in the hollow of his breast bone. The feel of the egg told him if the egg was fresh or rotten. After selecting only fifteen eggs, he paid the woman. Despite his test, that week a rotten egg still popped up and I could smell it all the way from the kitchen. I teased him about this. Then one day I decided to check his "feel" against my testing method of placing the eggs in a bowl of water. Some eggs that Jimmy thought were rotten sank in the water, while some eggs that he felt were good floated to the top. I let him decide which method to rely on.

On another occasion I had a chance to talk to the men. I wondered if they had heard about the war. I asked them if they had heard of Hitler. Every one knew of him:

"Oh, tha ba fellow."

"The ma who want to be Goh."

"When I see him, I kill him."

These were their reactions. I asked about Roosevelt, then Churchill, but no reaction. Then I asked them, if they knew Napoleon?

"A fighter."

"A Frenchman."

"The man who never says: I can try that, but I can do that."

Then Jimmy, my cook, who had listened to the conversation, came out of the kitchen and added with the authority of his French background,

"Uhung... Uhung...No trying palaver, but doing palaver...Uhung."

I thought it quite surprising that they had heard about these men and enjoyed their reactions.

This rainy season was unpredictable. Sometimes there were dry days, while at other times there were rainstorms early in the afternoon and then it was hot again. It was at this time that the flying ants' eggs would hatch. One evening we were sitting outside on the porch with the lamp on the table and, of course, the ants came flying towards the light. They were two-thirds wings and one-third body. John and Jimmy came out to catch the ants, either grabbing them in the air or taking them from the table. They stripped their wings and ate them alive. They were surprised that Hubert and I were watching them and they turned to us, saying: "Oh boh, fai, plenty grea!" (Oh boss, fine and plenty of grease.) When they had their fill they left. Suddenly we saw some little boys coming for their meal and we allowed them to catch the ants, but once in a while they choked on the wings. I wish I had a picture of this show. Then more people came with buckets of water and asked if they could set these around the table. In no time there were seven buckets. We watched the ants land on the table, walk some distance, lose their wings, and look for a spot to dig in. The people were busy shoving the ants into the buckets, where they floated on the water, and it was easier to scoop them up. The locals also fried these ants, which seemed to be a delicacy! I did not have the urge to taste the ants alive, but if they were fried and chocolate coated? Why not?

Later I read that a scientist, who had worked in Central Africa, had tried these young, hatched ants and been surprised by the taste, which was very similar to walnuts.

A year later, a young man dropped in to show us something strange. It was a large, white, slimy and transparent jelly mass about thirteen centimetres long, four centimetres wide and two and a half centimetres thick. It was quite dirty. There were some little ants around, the size of about half a centimetre. Suddenly I noticed that the mass had an ant's head at one end and at the other end a piece of an ant's tail. It was a monstrous sight to see. It was a queen ant and the queen was the real delicacy!

One evening after dark it was raining hard, but we knew that pretty soon the rain would stop, as it did most evenings. I had eaten my supper and John had finished washing the dishes and cleaning up. He came to the porch with his cap on, hands in his pockets and said that he had better wait a little longer until the rain stopped before going home. I could surely understand this. He walked to the corner of the porch, picked up the other easy chair, unfolded it, and placed it beside me. I thought how nice of him to do this for Theo. But instead, John settled himself in the chair and wanted to light a cigarette. I had to laugh, as I appreciated his innocence.

In the Liberian society the palaver house was in the centre of town, open on all sides. When a visitor or a dignitary came, the discussions were held in the palaver house and the townspeople, young and old, wandered in or stood just outside and listened to or took part in the conversations. It was a very open society, no secrets, no privacy. That was their culture.

I had to explain to John that I was used to inviting others before they sat down. John and I had travelled together and he had looked after me well. I liked him and I could trust him unconditionally, but I did not want to start socializing. That was my culture. With a deep sigh he reacted "Oh boss, white man has plenty law." Now, fifty years later, I wondered what we would have talked about.

Theo and I realized that we did not really fit the established hierachy of the company. We were responsible only to the general manager and because he was in New York or Holland half the time, we were actually independent. By day, I worked in the laboratory, getting the samples organized in trays for easy reference, making a glass model of the drilling of the ore body, tying all our maps together and guiding visitors to the outcrop.

There was drilling to be done in Monrovia at the harbour docks. It was to check the capacity of the subsoil for carrying structures and the ore, that was to be stored before loading. This job took me more than a month. A drill had been developed in the Dutch East Indies for tin sands, which could be operated by unskilled labor, using a number of men standing on the drill platform as weight. The company had bought one for eventualities and now it came in handy. There was an old pump to create the sludge. I used my expedition crew for this work. It was in the harbour compound and we drilled on the beach. There was no shade. At night, I had a constant headache. Suddenly it occured to me that I might get sunstroke. I bought a helmet and the headache disappeared. From then on I wore a helmet. Until that time I had not used a hat, as I had travelled in the bush, always under the shade of the trees.

During my stay in Monrovia I got to know more company employees. Two or three new families arrived every month and were added. They were stationed in the company compound in Brewerville, which was full of jealousy. I was glad when I could return to our harmonious community in Bomi Hills.

By the end of this rainy season I started to get itchy and I was anxious to go again on my way in the Interior. I felt under pressure to come up with an economical deposit somewhere, somehow.

The Fourth Expedition:
Tribulations of Locating the Promising Gold Vein

I started to realize that geology is a painstaking job and that the chances of coming up with a worthwhile find, were slim. But being an optimist, I never gave up hope. There were always gold flakes panned in the creeks and this was encouraging. I imagined that something would turn up at the moment I least expected it.

When the rainy season passed, I was on my way again. To get to my territory it was best to go to Boporo first, my staging point for the valleys to the north. The last time it had taken seven days to reach this town, but this time I chose a more direct route. Half way there I camped in the bush at an outcrop that I wanted to investigate. It was an hour from the town, so this saved me two hours of walking. My crew wanted to stay in town and left after camp was set up. After dinner John and Jimmy walked the extra hour, a distance which to them was nothing.

That night I was alone and it was quiet. After two hours, while I was sitting in the tent reading, I suddenly heard the noise of several animals. The tent flap was closed and I did not dare open it to see what the noise was all about, in case I would frighten the animals. I thought these might be bush cows, the most aggressive animals in the bush. Trembling, I took the shotgun and kept it on my lap, waiting. I realized that if the animals pushed the tent over, I would be wrapped in the canvas and would be unable to move. After some fifteen minutes, which seemed more than an hour to me, they moved on. That was the only time during my two years in Liberia that I was really scared. The following day I made arrangements for at least one man to always stay with me.

The only dangerous animals I encountered in the jungle were the bush cows, leopards, snakes and crocodiles. The monkey population in the area where I travelled was scarce, though Theo met monkey colonies quite regularly on his travels. Our hunter shot monkeys and deer, although I never saw deer. I was told that, because of the noise I made, the animals moved away.

Anyhow, we reached Boporo safely and continued on. Travelling past Boporo we came to a ridge that we had to cross to reach the next valley. Daniel, our hunter-headman, led the way, while I followed in the rear taking samples and making notes on the topography. After about eight hours we came to a fork in the trail, where Daniel met two native hunters. He had to wait until there was a man who could understand these hunters. He heard that it was still far to go to town, though we could be there before dark. The natives were nice and saw that we were thirsty, so they shared some cola nuts with the crew. John told me that I should also eat half a nut, because they were good for thirst and we shared one. It tasted bitter, but my thirst disappeared and it gave us a boost. We continued and indeed before dark we walked into a small settlement of about nine huts, after having travelled for twelve hours. Then we heard there was no rice in town. We were accustomed to being able to secure food in the towns we passed through and consequently, to keep the loads as light as possible, our party did not carry any rice. What next?

To add to the problem, a storm was brewing. I heard non-stop rumbling the whole afternoon. The town chief told Dean that I could use the palaver house as my living quarters and kitchen. The crew were quartered in the different huts. But by nightfall we still had not received any rice from the chief and none of our crew ate. I also did not eat, though Jimmy wanted to dig into my canned supplies. I did not think that fair.

I put pressure on the chief and the town elders by showing them a pass our company received, that was signed and sealed by the president of Liberia. It said that the local authorities were to supply us with required carriers and rice. Until now there had been no need to use this pass, but in this emergency I did. It did not feel good pressuring these people for their scarce food and I decided, then and there, that I would never again be caught without rice.

In the meantime, the rumbling became stronger and stronger. The elders went to see what they could do about the rice. I was left with my cook and steward. Suddenly the wind started to blow, the temperature dropped, my cook and steward disappeared and I was alone in the palaver house in a sandstorm that later changed to rain. In the palaver house, open on all sides, there was no hiding. I did not know what to do and it got so cold that I went to bed in my khaki clothes under the two blankets.

After half an hour, the old chief came with some rice and found me lying in bed.

The next morning Dean found out where we would likely be able to get rice, but it involved two days travel. Dean and I picked our four fastest, most trusted carriers and with a lot of incentives, including money, sent them on their mission. In the meantime, I continued prospecting with the crew, tightened my belt a notch, kept focused on the work and stayed away from food. Three days later the first carriers returned with one hundred pounds of rice. Every man got his ration and all were glad.

Apparently the natives were used to going without food at times because nobody complained. I had experienced being without food twice in Holland during the long war winters of 1941 and 1944. I had learned that as long as you did not think about food, you could handle the hunger. We stayed four days in this town until we were well supplied with rice and then we continued north.

Three days later we reached a valley and settled in a gold camp. I was interested in the cliff at the side of the valley, where I expected the mother lode of gold. The chief of the gold camp was a Madingo. The Madingos were Muslims. At night I heard them outside praying to Allah. This camp had three huts for the Madingo families and an empty bunkhouse for about fifteen diggers, so my crew was accommodated there. My tent was erected just outside the camp in a clearing. The local custom was to keep a good-size border around the huts cleaned, to reduce the flow of bugs.

The first day there was trouble. It was about two hours before dark when I noticed that a stream of ants were headed for the tent. I called John to get some workers to make fires to keep these ants away. John told me that I did not have to worry. He had heard that the Madingo chief had power over these ants and he would ask him to take care of them.

Indeed, fifteen minutes later, the chief came in his beautiful blue robe. He had the Koran in his left hand and a huge knife in its sheath in the belt around his waist. He opened the Koran and recited some passages loudly. Then he took the knife out of the sheath, spat on it and used it to draw a circle around the tent. He said to me, "You won't have any more trouble," and left. I said to John that this did not look too good and he had better stay around. But John replied that I did not have to worry because the chief had taken care of the ant problem. He went away, convinced.

There was nothing for me to do but to take my chair and watch the ants approach the tent. When the ants reached the cut line, they hesitated, crawled over the edge, came down in that little ditch, turned around and walked away! The ants had been coming from all the sides, but no ants came into the tent that night. I watched the whole performance with interest, having observed the actions of the chief in detail. Eventually, convinced that I was safe from an ant invasion, I went to bed.

It was now a weekly routine to send a runner to Bomi Hills with a progress report for head office, allowing three days to get there, one day in Bomi Hills and three days to return, a total of seven days. The second runner left, after the first runner returned, but this time the second runner did not return on time. After ten days we realized something was wrong. We were running out of supplies. On the twelfth day Dean and I decided to send John to Bomi Hills. Five days later he returned with the news. The second carrier had walked day and night until he reached a small town close to Bomi Hills, all the runners did this. There he stayed with friends for five days. Then he realized that he was expected back in our camp the next day. He went to Bomi Hills early in the morning, got the supplies, mail and money and returned to the town of his friends. On the way he opened the money bag and started partying. He later disappeared, leaving the letters scattered in the bush. One of the townspeople found the letters and gave them to John. This was the only time in Liberia that I had an untrustworthy employee.

During this time while we were short on supplies, Jimmy managed to prepare simple meals: rice pancakes fried in palm oil in the morning and rice with chicken in the afternoon. I could certainly survive on this.

I stayed three weeks longer. First I panned the creek for gold and then did quite a bit of work on the slope of the valley, tracing the flakes up the hill.

My entertainment at the end of the day was reading, and watching the dancing when there was a full moon and, of course, watching the ants and the chickens. One Sunday I was relaxing outside the tent reading, when John brought me coffee. It was mid-morning. Around me chickens were pecking for their food, constantly turning their heads and aiming their eyes at the sky. I had not realized that their eyes could not move to look up to the sky and that the only way to keep track of the hawks was by turning their heads. Suddenly, there was a lot of cackling. The chickens ran away, one chicken was lifted from the ground by a hawk, but it was too heavy and the hawk dropped it. After a few muscle jerks, the chicken was dead.

The dead chicken lay at the edge of the clearing. After some ten minutes I looked up from my book and saw a small stream of ants heading towards the chicken. Ten minutes later, there were four highways of ants, six rows wide, moving in on the chicken. Within half an hour all of the flesh of that chicken was gone, but the ant stream continued. After two more hours there was no sign of the chicken. Everything was gone: bones, feathers, nails and the beak.

During this stay I observed the attitudes and customs of the people. It seemed an easy life, in which men and women were uninhibited. The leadership was male: the town chief, clan chief and paramount chief. Typical male jobs were hunting, weaving and tailoring. The women picked and cleaned the rice, hauled water, cooked meals and fished. Burning the forest for planting and building the huts appeared to be communal activities.

We continued our search for the source of the gold. We had traced the flakes on the slope of the valley and plotting these flakes on a map, it showed as a funnel shaped pattern that pointed to a spot of an almost vertical, overgrown cliff, about twenty metres high. We were on the right track. We had to clean a trench on this cliff. It was easier to make this trench from the top down and we found a trail to the top. Here, Dean showed us how to make a ladder. He located a type of vine and used two pieces as frame, along with sticks for steps and twigs for rope, assembling a flexible ladder that would follow the contours of the cliff. We carried the rolled-up ladder to the edge of the cliff and unrolled this over the edge, then cleared a narrow trench down the cliff. When checking this trench in late afternoon, I was half-way down the cliff, where I spotted a quartz vein and what I thought was a gold reflection. Remembering my first experience, I quickly chipped off a piece and planned to return the next day.

Back at camp, I found a letter from our general manager, asking me to be back in Monrovia before his departure to New York. This letter had taken three weeks to reach me. I had only four days to get back to Monrovia. It was already three in the afternoon. Dean and I immediately went back to the outcrop and just before dark we took proper samples. After completing this we hurried home, but on the way to our camp, we got caught by darkness.

In the jungle, travelling away from the normal path, we would make our own trail by cutting branches with a cutlass or breaking the branches out of the way of the trail. This served to find the way back by day. Now, we had to find our way by feeling these cut or broken branches. It was pitch dark and very slow going. Every so often we felt another cut or broken branch and we knew that we were on the right trail. We advanced a few metres at a time, holding each other. We expected that our headman Daniel would come to look for us after dark. Finally we heard Daniel and his crew coming and they caught up to us, carrying lanterns. Late that night Dean and I were having our dinner, discussing the next move.

With John and another strong carrier, I left early the following morning, heading east. I intended to reach the main highway from Monrovia to French Guinea, where I could organize transportation to Monrovia. This was the only way to make it there before the general manager's departure. We had to travel between ten and twelve hours each day, hoping to find trails leading to the highway. Dean, in the meantime, would return with the crew to Bomi Hills.

On the third day, we reached the coastal plain, which was hilly, with no trees, but straight roads. At midday we spotted, a few kilometres away, two dots coming toward us, one white and one black. If we were on top of a hill, we could not see them, when they were in a valley. But then they would appear again, every time getting bigger and bigger, until we could clearly see two men, a hunter and his helper. Of course I got excited. For seven or eight weeks I had not heard any news. We came closer, one hundred metres, fifty metres, ten metres and then we passed, just saying hello. I could not stand it any longer and I turned around and said that I had to talk. I told the hunter I was on my way to Monrovia and had been in the Interior for two months. Apparently, he understood my feelings. He explained that he was from the U.S. Economic Mission and having a day off, figured he might as well do some hunting. That was enough of a conversation for me and we each continued. Later that day, I organized a truck. That night we reached Monrovia, where I was dropped off at our company guest-house.

The next morning I went to the office to see the general manager and delivered my report and samples. We discussed the work. He left for New York, leaving the samples in the office. Because of the hurried departure to Monrovia, there was no time to follow the quartz vein. It was unfinished prospecting. Had I found my gold vein?

One year later somebody found these samples laying in the corner of the office. Sent to the U.S. for gold assaying, the results came back. The samples were evaluated at more than seven hundred dollars per ton, an extremely high value at that time. The market price of gold was thirty-five dollars per ounce, guaranteed by the U.S. government.

Nobody expected that, not even me.

The Fifth Expedition:
The Health Aspect became my
Public Relation Trump

The systematic investigation of our concession continued to ensure that we did not miss anything of importance. On this expedition the contents of my medicine box was more effective in healing wounds then the efforts of the local witch-doctor. It became my public relation trump card.

After returning from Monrovia, I found Dean and the crew already in Bomi Hills. I paid them their savings. Then I ordered replenishments of our supplies. When these arrived we returned to the north-east, again taking the trail to Boporo. In a little village, an army of ants attacked my tent. I figured I could imitate the Madingo chief. I went to the kitchen and asked Jimmy for the biggest kitchen knife he had. I slipped it under my belt. Returning to the tent I took my economic geology book and placed myself in approximately the same position as the chief had taken in relation to the sun. Like the chief, who read from the Koran, I read a paragraph from my economic geology book. Then I pulled out the kitchen knife, spit on the blade and drew a line around the tent. In surprise, John watched me. I explained that I was creating similar conditions to what our Madingo chief had done, to order the ants' retreat. I took my chair and watched the ant stream continue their attack on the tent, undisturbedly crossing the line which I had made with the knife. I did not possess the magic power of the Madingo chief. I moved away from the tent, acknowledged my incompetence and read until the ants completed their scrounging in the tent. Apparently my analytical observations had missed an important step.

An ant stream is fascinating to watch. A few ants go in one direction, then more and more join until there is a highway of ants marching six abreast, slowly moving the sand sideways and up. A quarter of an hour later, the ants return on top of the outgoing stream, carrying something in their mouths. If attracted by food, they come from several directions. Eventually, when faced with an ant attack on the tent, hut or house, we learned to let them have their way. At night, the simplest way was to move a chair and a table outside, take a book and wait until the ants cleared out all the eatables. When they finished, all the bugs and mice were gone. The ants marched away as suddenly as they came.

Four days after my failure with the ants we entered a town. At the edge of town a group of women stood with their skirts spread out and their backs toward the road. Later on I heard a baby was being delivered. That night after dinner, I was asked to visit a sick girl. When I came into the hut, a number of women were sitting around the bed, where the girl lay. She seemed to be in pain. I checked her forehead, which was hot. Her pulse was racing, she had a high fever. I thought I smelled something rotten. Then I heard she had just delivered a healthy baby. What does a mining engineer do in a delivery room?

I went back to the medicine box but, of course, there was nothing written on the bottles about infection after delivery. I figured aspirin and sulphonamide tablets could not do any harm. Two days later, the women buried her, packed in palm leaves. I felt sad.

A few months later I met a doctor from the Firestone plantation and asked him what I should have done. He said that perhaps three times the dosage I had given could have helped the girl, but you never can tell. From him I heard that in a delivery, when the baby does not come easy, the women take a round log and roll it over the abdomen to press the baby out. Of course, this often resulted in internal damage. The treatment was also unhygienic and infection could occur.

In these towns were many young children with hernias, some sticking one to two centimetres out of their belly button. I wondered if it was done on purpose or was the result of a botched delivery. Of course there were no statistics on birthing. I had no idea how high the infant mortality rate was. Many young women walked around looking pregnant, but it was easy for me to mistake a rice belly for pregnancy. The local population had only one meal a day, consisting of about one pound of rice per person.

One day Dean told me that a baby had been born and the chief had asked him if I could prepare a birth certificate, which would be the first one in town. I agreed, but I needed the names of the baby and the parents. Nobody knew the father's name. I realized then that relationships were loose and most people had no idea how old they actually were.

When I entered the next village, all the children ran away. The people in this district had never seen a white man. Even the chickens and sheep seemed to realize that something strange was going on. A young girl, perhaps fourteen, saw me coming and she ran away, yelling, as if she had seen the devil, until she reached her mother, who laughed. Later that night the children painted their faces white with laterite clay, which could be found readily in most tropical countries and which was used to whitewash the bottom of huts.

Because this relatively sizeable town of about seventy huts was more or less in the center of the north-east region, in which I was interested, we used it as our staging point. Every time we passed through, we were able to replenish our requirements of rice and palm oil. Also our weekly dispatcher could easily locate us on his return from Bomi Hills.

One day a hunter came to Jimmy with two really big eggs. Jimmy asked if I wanted to buy these eggs at ten cents each. He assured me they were good! The eggs were long and heavy, almost the size of my hand, with a darker strip along the length. They were alligator eggs. I agreed, so Jimmy cooked the eggs and John placed them on a plate in front of me. The moment I cracked the shell, the stench was horrible—both eggs were rotten. John came right away and asked if he and Jimmy could have the eggs. For them it seemed to be a delicacy.

The following week we stopped in this town again. After Dean held the first-aid session, he called me to examine an older woman with a scarf on her head. After taking it off, I could see her head was full of scabs. I thought that she wore a scarf to hide the scabs. I figured it could be scurvy. In the medicine box was a bottle labelled scurvy, with an explanation on treatment. The first step was to have her hair cut as short as possible and wash her head with Superol. Afterward I made sure the haircutter washed her hands thoroughly. Using a spatula, I covered the woman's head with the ointment from the bottle and bandaged her as well as I could. I told her to put a clean scarf over the bandage.

After the weekend, before we left town, I figured I better have a look at that woman. Most of the scabs had disappeared and her head looked much healthier, but the scarf was dirty again. I repeated the treatment and told her to boil the scarf and put on a clean one. I packed the medicine box and washed my hands. Just when I turned to walk away, I saw the woman putting the dirty scarf on her young daughter's head. I stopped her immediately and the interpreter made sure she understood what I was saying. Through him, I gave a sermon on hygiene and on the possibility of contagion. I made it sound a little worse than I really thought it would be, to make a deep impression. Nevertheless, I was not sure that after three days it would be remembered, as everybody scratched their head with dirty fingers.

I moved to the next valley, which was overgrown with underbrush and loaded with red and black ants. After cutting a trail through the threatening brush, we came to a hidden creek. Beside the creek was a hut with a family. Out of the hut came two little children, perhaps five and seven years old. They had a very light skin, reddish hair and reddish eyes. I noticed their bodies were full of sores. This was the first time I saw albinos. I got the feeling this family was ostracized and had to make it on their own without tribal support. I wondered if this was a form of reverse discrimination.

After investigating this valley, I returned to the same town. Word had got around that the white man with his medicine box could cure some problems that the local witch-doctor was unable to handle and the treatment was free. Dean held the first-aid session, administering liniment and treating cuts. There was a big crowd of people. At the end of the first-aid session, a boy of about fifteen was shoved in front and I was asked to have a look at him. He needed a stick to move. Hobbling, he settled on the trunk of a fallen tree. On his leg just under his knee, was a horrible tropical sore, about the size of a fist, with pus running out of the wound. First, I cleaned around it with rubbing alcohol, the only disinfecting agent in the medicine box. Then, I sprinkled sulphonamide on it, bandaged it as well as I could and told the boy not to take a bath for some days. He left and I forgot about the case.

We kept working in the area and after several days again returned to the same town. The boy showed up, still hobbling on his stick. The wound was almost closed, but there was still some infection in the centre. However it looked considerably better and I repeated the treatment.

We stayed in this district another week and when I returned to the town, I was interested to see how the sore on the knee of that boy would look, but the boy was gone.

One evening after dinner John came and said there was a man who wanted to see me. I was always a little annoyed by such a request, but I had nothing else to do, so I agreed to see him. Along came an old man with a white chicken, a pound of white rice and the boy, who by now was limping only slightly without a stick. The man wanted me to see that the wound had healed completely. He had walked for a day to come and thank me. He said that his boy had had the sore for two years and no previous treatment would cure it. They had used the local medicine of some special dirt, but the sore had not healed. After that, some spider webs were applied, but these did not help either. The wound got worse and the boy became more disabled. I thanked the man for the chicken, felt moved and reciprocated by giving him tobacco leaves. I was glad that John used his judgement and had not sent the man away.

We soon discovered that in this sparsely populated area, the locals were unable to sustain the demands of our crew and food became a problem. Luckily, I had put aside some rice for an emergency. Travelling home, we reached Boporo, the district's town. Even here they were short of rice. I was able to issue half a pound of rice to each of my carriers, while I took a can of beans.

After the meal, I was called to the sister of the paramount chief, a woman of middle age. She told me that she was ill with a fever. Three days previously, she had walked quite some distance and now she was stiff, tired and sick. I checked her pulse, but she was so fat I could not feel the beat until I put my fingers along her neck. It was normal. I could help her. For her stiffness, I prescribed some vitamin pills. For her tiredness, I figured a quinine pill every day for three days would not harm her. I went back to the tent and the thought occurred to me that the family very likely could afford to pay for the medicine in rice. I figured that one pound of rice for each pill would be enough. I sent my foreman to negotiate this and without difficulty he received the payment.

During this year I had noticed progress in the Interior. There was more varied merchandise in the store such as pots and pans and even two bottles of Heineken beer. The prices were ridiculous, but I had been in the bush for more than a month and had not spent a nickel on myself. Our expedition was on its way to our base camp at Bomi Hills. That morning we had already travelled five hours and I was soaking wet with perspiration. I was thirsty and the beer looked good. I knew it was not the right thing to do, but I bought the two bottles. I treated myself and drank them. The beer tasted wonderful, but five minutes after finishing it, I was as drunk as a skunk. My crew was ahead of me, so I had to continue. Singing loudly and soaking wet, I marched on. Half an hour later the beer had worked itself through my system and I started to sober up, realizing that soon my good feelings would be over and then what?

That day we had still another six hours to go for some eleven hours total, our goal being Bomi Hills with its familiar conveniences. Late that afternoon we arrived and I found the mail from home.

Exploration-wise I had covered a sizeable segment of our concession beyond Boporo, although I had not discovered anything significant in this area. On the other hand, the company had created goodwill among the people in these far-away valleys by always compensating them for services rendered and with the odd bit of medical assistance. I hoped this news would slowly travel in the hinterland and might eventually be of benefit.

The Sixth Expedition:
Confronted with Black Magic

The magic of Africa often sounded like the stories of the gypsy seers or the tarot-card readers. Everyone who visited Liberia heard about the "sassy wood," the stick that tells the truth. And the local population swore by it.

This time, on my sixth expedition, we stopped in a very small village of eight huts. In the morning John could not find my magnifier. He looked through my luggage three times with no luck. We tried to recall when was the last time I had used it and where I had last seen it. I tried to reconstruct all the possibilities of the previous day. Was it lost, had it been stolen, or was it mislaid? I needed this tool daily to identify rocks.

In desperation John asked the townspeople and the town chief. Half an hour later, the town chief came back to him, proposing to "play the sassy wood." I had heard about this, when, on my way from Monrovia to Bomi Hills, I had stayed overnight with the survey crew in Clay. Our two surveyors had watched a performance after some tools had gone missing. Having been told about the "sassy wood," they wanted to witness a session. Though they did not really believe in it, they were willing to put up the necessary money. Their headman contacted the town chief and found out that the medicine man was prepared to "play the sassy wood." After negotiating with the medicine man, the price was established at three dollars. The performance would take place early the following morning.

The medicine man bought, on credit, some cane juice, a potent alcoholic drink. He and his friends started drinking that afternoon. Soon, a drummer appeared and the dancing started. A few hours later the town party was in full swing. It lasted deep into the night and kept the survey crew awake.

The next morning, very early, the medicine man disappeared into the bush and reappeared with the sassy-wood stick an hour later. It was daybreak. Everybody in town had to come to the town square. A fire was prepared and a cutlass placed in the fire with a bucket of water beside it. The medicine man sat in front of the fire with the sassy wood in his hands and started singing. The singing changed to crying and then yelling and after about half an hour it seemed that he hardly knew what he was doing. He was sweating and his face was distorted. Suddenly he sat down. There was complete silence. He walked up to the fire, took out the cutlass, which was now red-hot at one end, took the wet cloth out of the bucket and walked up to where all the men stood together in a group. One by one, he wet one of each man's legs with the cloth and then, with the red-hot cutlass, came so close to this leg that it sizzled. Not a man moved his leg, demonstrating complete trust. He then came to a man who showed no confidence and was nervous. The medicine man wet this man's leg and came close with the red-hot cutlass. The man suddenly tried to withdraw his leg, but the red-hot cutlass was pressed against it, making a nasty burn. The man confessed to the stealing and the stolen tools were returned. The medicine man was paid and the population was convinced of the sassy wood's power. My friends on the survey crew thought that the party the previous night had provided the medicine man with the information he needed to identify the culprit. How else could he have selected the right man?

This sassy-wood play seemed a kind of a voodoo, and it did not fit into the rational thinking of a mining engineer from Holland. However, I was intrigued to see what this was all about. In the village, where we were staying, the chief said there was a sassy-wood player. The townspeople were notified that a play would be held in the area between the huts. Everybody, young and old, including my crew and myself, had to attend. In total, there were some seventy people.

The sassy-wood player, a middle-aged man, set himself behind a wooden tub filled with water. In his hands were three sassy-wood sticks that he had just cut in the forest. He worked himself up into a frenzy and after a quarter of an hour he was in a trance, shaking like a reed and foaming at the mouth. When he was ready, or when the town chief thought he was ready, the town chief walked to the centre of the square and started to ask questions:

"Is the object in the tent of the white man?" The sticks moved, agitated, horizontally, which meant, "no."

"Is the object in the white man's kitchen?" The sticks moved horizontally again, "no."

"Is the object in town?" The sticks, again indicated, "no."

"Did the object come into town?" The sticks again said, "no."

"Did somebody steal the object?" The sticks again, "no."

After a few more insignificant questions, the town chief gave up. I gave the player his dash for the services. I decided to send our headman back for one day's travel, to look for the magnifier, while I continued with the expedition. He could catch up to us a day later.

When we had left, our headman talked with the townspeople and they told him that their sassy-wood player was not a good one, but in the next town, a bigger town, there was a good sassy-wood player. Our headman was so convinced of the power of the sassy-wood play that he decided, instead of going back, as we had discussed that his chances of success would be much improved if he went and saw that sassy-wood player. After one day's walking, he came to the next town and that night, with the better sassy-wood player, he got the answer: he and the white man had rested beside a creek and left the object there.

The following day the headman walked back to the town where we had parted and stayed there overnight. The next day he returned to the creek where we had sat down and panned for gold. There he met a hunter, who had arrived a short time before him and found the magnifier. The hunter was contemplating what to do with it. Our headman gave him enough money to get the magnifier back.

But now he was about three days behind our expedition and of course, we had continued our travel. Eventually he caught up with us and told me of his experiences.

Then I remembered that day vividly. We had travelled some eight hours and stopped by a creek for testing.

Panning for gold at a creek crossing

We met some people on the trail and they told us we still had far to go. By that time my water-bottle was empty and I was thirsty. I did not know if the water in that creek was potable. There were two safe and practical ways to quench my thirst. The easiest way was to use a vine, cutting a sizeable piece of about an arm thick and holding it vertical, draining the liquid into a cup. But there were no vines in this spot. I had to make use of the other well-known remedy, which was to put my wrists into the stream. The cooling effect reduced the feeling of thirst. In doing this, I had to bend over the water with my magnifier dangling. Instead, I had taken it off my neck. After I had cooled off, I was distracted and did not remember to pick up the magnifier.

Was I ever glad to have my magnifier back! This was an expensive and inconvenient lesson.

Financial Worries

In a small mining enterprise, fortunes go up and down with the success of the leadership, fluctuations in the market price of the product, or political and economic developments in the country.

At the end of 1948, the financial situation of our company became precarious. As employees, we did not know the details, but we were all advised that, as of January 1, 1949, the activities of the company would be reduced by two-thirds. Rumours were that our president hoped to get a steel company involved to assist in financing, while allowing him to retain control. So far he had been unsuccessful and he was running out of funds. How would that affect us, the employees?

It was a sad story. Just as I got an efficient team together, I had to send them home. All staff employees were expected to be in Brewerville a week before Christmas. The company compound in Brewerville now had fifteen bungalows and the staff had grown to about twenty men. The wives of half of them had already arrived in Liberia.

The day after I arrived in Brewerville, I discovered that I was the only one in the company to receive an embossed invitation from the foreign secretary to attend a New Year's reception and ball. I had no idea why I received that invitation. It was the assistant manager who should represent our company. He must have wanted to stay home for political or financial reasons and so passed the honour on to me. I thought it would be interesting to attend and I felt like representing the company.

When it was time for the reception, I left for Monrovia. Of course I asked Jordense what to wear. I dressed in a white shirt with a tie, a pair of white pants and a jacket. The company car drove me to the foreign affairs' building. Going up the steps, I was directed to a very large reception hall. At the far end stood the minister, his wife and a general. I shook hands and wished them a happy new year. Then I walked to one side, where I saw some acquaintances from the waterfront stores. All of the black men were in formal dress: black tails, striped pants and black tie. Most of the white men were dressed in a sports jacket, white pair of pants, white shirt and a very colorful tie. We were invited to come to the centre of the reception hall, where the minister read a proclamation, which I could not hear for all the noise. After he finished, the audience clapped politely. The guests were told that refreshments were set up on the side tables and suddenly I realized that the Liberian national anthem was being played by the home guard, because all the Liberians stood at attention. Then we all shook hands with the Liberians and wished them a happy new year. While we were shaking hands, the soldiers slipped in and poured all the glasses with our drinks into a big one and drank it, a mixture of beer, Coca-Cola, whiskey and punch. Some people even had their drinks grabbed from their hands. After this episode everybody left, to return later. That evening I changed into a tuxedo, which I had borrowed from one of our staff employees, and I was driven back to the same building. Again I entered the large room, and again at the far end were the minister, his wife and the general. The opening of the ball started with a real polonaise, the minister and his wife led the parade, followed by members of the diplomatic corps and the other invited guests, all with their ladies on their arm. They paraded to the music of "Silent Night," played in the tempo of the marches of Sousa. Then the dancing started. I enjoyed myself admiring the dresses of the ladies, and I realized that these officials were now able to walk for more than fifteen minutes. When they had been in the countryside, they had needed a hammock for even the shortest distance. At last we were invited to the roof garden, where there was a nice cool sea breeze. Two searchlights and loudspeakers had been installed. The home guard band played Charles Trenet's "Boum," a minuet, "The Hokey Pokey" and the waltzes of Strauss. The black people were sitting on one side and the white people on the other. I wanted to dance and I invited a black lady, who was alone at a table. She accepted reluctantly, but after one dance, that was it. I learned my lesson not to invite other black ladies to dance. I wished I knew more people. It was after midnight when the car arrived and I went home.

In Liberia, extremes were side-by-side. After the New Year's reception I returned to Brewerville and the next day I took the jeep to have a look at a mica outcrop in the countryside. Suddenly the jeep's motor stalled. I could not get it started without a push. An older native walked by, who was perhaps forty-five years old, fresh from the bush, wearing only a loin cloth and carrying a long spear. A naked little boy, about five years old and very likely his son, followed him. I asked the man to give me a push, but of course he did not understand me. After a lot of gesturing, he at last got the idea and gave me a push. I got the clutch into third gear and luckily the jeep started. Then I gestured to the man that I would give him a ride to town. He and his son got into the jeep, the man standing straight up. I waved for him to sit down, but he interpreted that as meaning to jump out of the car. I got out and, standing beside him, I gestured for him and his boy to sit in the car. I pushed him down into a seated position in the back seat, ran around the vehicle, got behind the wheel and, before he could jump out again, drove them into town. He was laughing and laughing loudly, his spear proudly upright in his hand. I don't think he had ever ridden in a car before. His little boy held his head in his hands, huddling against his father. I dropped them off in a little village not far from Brewerville. This event was such a contrast to the formal New Year's party with long dresses and black tie and the European music, two days earlier.

I celebrated in Brewerville the New Year again with the staff.

At the beginning of 1949, the explorations of the concession were cancelled. I was transferred to the railroad team, where I designed a railroad bridge for the ore trains over the Kpo River. Fortunately, there were good reference books and I finished the job in a month. A year and a half later the railroad bridge was being installed.

Bridge being installed across the Kpo River

We heard that a U.S. steel company was interested in the iron deposit and would visit Bomi Hills. The people in Bomi Hills were instructed to "dress up" the deposit. As Theo had fallen ill, I was called from

Brewerville to assist. I had no notion what was meant by "dressing up," but I assumed I would find out. I was asked to take along ten boxes of dynamite and to pick up nine boxes of supplies at the waterfront stores in Monrovia. Early in the morning, with a crew of ten men, I took off in a pick-up truck. By noon we were at the end of the almost completed truck road. From there it was a four-hour walk to Bomi Hills. It was the dry season and the locals were burning the bush to clear for rice planting. I did not want to leave the dynamite boxes along the road under these circumstances, so I asked the town chief if my supply boxes could be left with him for storage. We took the dynamite boxes with us. Walking through the countryside, it was clear that the burning caused erosion. We arrived safely in Bomi Hills. The next day my crew went back to pick up the boxes of supplies.

The superintendent and I walked the trails along the outcrop, laying these out in a manner so that the outcrop was seen from the most favourable angles. We discovered that an outcrop looks more impressive viewed from the bottom up, rather then from the top down. The trails were improved for easy walking. When a trail went around a corner, showing a new view, we painted the tonnage of that area on the rock. In other spots we cleared the forest so that our visitors would have an impressive view of the deposit. Of course we eliminated the areas where there was not much to see. We achieved remarkable effects. From the top of Monkey Hill, the visitor had a grandiose view of the countryside. We figured he would be impressed by the height and magnitude of the ore body. In the camp the broken down trucks were cleaned and placed beside all the other equipment. I think we made good preparations for a selling job.

Our company and Mueller and Co. from Rotterdam had together financed the development work to date. Our company president had tried to get many American steel companies interested, but there were other rich iron-ore deposits on the world market at that time. For him, time was running out and the financing might dry up completely.

The first party that visited Bomi Hills was the Stettinius group. They seemed to be business oriented. After they left, they sent a photographer to prepare pictures for their brochures. I guided both parties to the outcrop and back to Monrovia.

The next party was the Republic Steel Company. Our president had an expert adviser, Dr T.P.(Tom)Thayer, on his team. Tom was a top geologist with the U.S. Geological Survey and had visited Bomi Hills in 1943 during the war. Republic Steel came with a party of seven men, of which two were geologists, two were mining engineers and two were EX-IM (Export Import Bank) officials. I guided these men around, but of course was not part of their negotiations. Apparently Republic Steel was interested.

A week after the Republic Steel party left Bomi Hills, I got malaria, a most serious and devastating tropical sickness. The company staff was supplied with quinine pills. A well-known side effect of using quinine was that your ears started buzzing. New drugs, Atabrine and Paludrine, were introduced to eliminate these side effects. We used to swallow quinine for one week, then Atabrine for the next week and finally a week of Paludrine. This rotation of drugs seemed to work. Paludrine was an easy drug to take, as you needed only one hundred milligrams once a week. But, as a typical young man, I had started to skip, or rather forget, taking the pills regularly and, when nothing happened, I thought it was not that important anyway. as I did not see any mosquitoes flying around.

This time I became incredibly sick. I could not walk and passed out. Theo and Hubert decided they better send me on to the doctor in Monrovia. Theo arranged transportation by hammock to where a truck could pick me up. I was so sick that I did not remember anything about this trip, which was the only hammock ride I took in Liberia.

The hammock was strung to a long pole, at each end tied to a board. It required four carriers. I weighed about eighty kilograms, which meant about twenty kilograms per carrier, so there had to be a spare crew.

Later on I heard that the carriers had ran for about four hours, to where the truck road was completed. There waited a pick-up truck, which took me to the company compound in Brewerville. Here I was transferred into the jeep of the assistant manager, who happened to go to Monrovia and who would drop me off at the hospital. On the way to Monrovia we had a flat tire. The two of us changed the tire, although I was groggy and had a 104 degree fever. I did not think the assistant manager had ever changed a tire before. He dropped me off at the hospital. How long I was there and what they did to me, I have no idea.

After recovering from this sickness I returned to Bomi Hills, where I heard there were tough, ongoing negotiations with Republic Steel.

During this time the differences in remuneration between the Liberians, the Europeans and the Americans became apparent. When I engaged Dean as an overseer, I paid him twenty-five dollars a month, about ten times the basic wage of the unskilled labor force. A year later, when the American geologists joined our team, they raised his pay by one hundred dollars, to the same level as a European foreman, as he did the same type of work.

Working in an international organization, the disparities became evident. People from Holland were paid well compared to the salary scale at home at that time after the war. However, the workers from Holland were getting only one-third of what the Americans received. Besides nationality considerations, there were also political ones. We employed a man at the dynamite compound, who was supposed to control the dynamite issue. His salary was twenty-five dollars per month. His brother was a cabinet minister who had important dealings with our company. When this brother, the minister, met our president, there must have been pressure, because suddenly the man's salary was increased to one hundred and twenty-five dollars per month. When I met our dynamite supervisor at the official New Year's function, his uniform was loaded with ribbons.

There were also cultural differences. The spoken languages, English and tribal, were enriched with gestures. Hand and finger gestures were often used to enhance communications: Pointing to the side of my forehead indicated that I was thinking; pointing with my index finger to my nose indicated smelling; pointing to my eyes indicated seeing; and holding my hand behind my ears indicated listening. When I wanted something or somebody to come to me, I put my hand in front of my chest and rotated my hand down to my stomach, opposite to what I was used to.

In Monrovia there were two ways to shake hands. If I knew the person casually, I shook his hand. However, if a Liberian knew me well and wanted to express appreciation, he would shake my hand and then withdrawing his hand, squeeze with his fingers and the palm of his hand. If done forcefully by both parties at the same time, it sounded like a snap, the louder, the dearer.

Another cultural difference was that Liberian officials were never called by their first name, the same as in Europe, while the Americans seemed to feel uncomfortable if their first name was not used immediately. For me a first-name basis was only reserved for the person I knew very well.

The economic conditions in Liberia were risky, but healthy profits were possible. The bank, owned by Firestone, was aware of the profits that could be made with the rubber plantations. The coffee plantations seemed to provide a return of about forty percent and so did the vegetable oil industry, with the local price of oil being sixty four dollars per barrel, while the world price was around four hundred dollars. I heard that the royalties of the iron ore were low at five cents per ton, while the world price was four dollars per ton. It was estimated that the return on investment of our mine would be between twenty-five and thirty percent. Was that enough of an enticement? Republic Steel had the money and the know-how and needed the ore, our president had the concession and the Liberians owned the deposit.

When Republic Steel took an option to finance the undertaking, the relief was made very palatable by the company president. He gave a ten percent raise across the board to all staff employees for staying with the company during this turbulent situation. I think that only the general manager was aware of the predicament the president had been in.

Three months after the financing was in place, the prospecting started up again.

The Seventh Expedition:
The Eastern Province

After Republic Steel committed resources to Bomi Hills, our president went after the other known iron deposit in the country, this one in the Tchien district of the Eastern Province, some six hundred kilometres north-east of Monrovia. The company obtained the rights to that deposit, as well as the right to investigate the gold deposits in that area. I was assigned to this expedition.

In the office, the assistant manager, Jordense and I discussed the implications of this reconnaissance expedition. Jordense, the know-it-all, had travelled through this district before. He thought the expedition might take a month or so. It was August and he thought it was possible to squeeze the expedition in during the dry spell in the middle of this rainy season, a decision which later turned out to be very risky.

Of course, Dean and John would go along. Jordense, through his contacts, heard that carriers were available in Gbanga, so I did not have to bring my crew from Bomi Hills. We needed carriers to move from one major town to the next one. We anticipated that there were few or no carriers available in the villages. To have the utmost flexibility, I reduced supplies to the bare minimum, so I would need only ten carriers. John had to double up as cook. I intended to locate an interpreter locally.

The money was decided and the safety angle was discussed. I felt safe in this country. We carried a hunting gun used for deer and monkeys. My experience was that I did not need a revolver for protection.

To reach Tchien we could travel by truck to Gbanga, about four hundred and fifty kilometres away, using the existing all-weather road into French Guinea. Jordense located a truck that could take us along on its way north. From there it was another two hundred kilometres or five days on foot to Tchien, the capital of the Eastern Province. Jordense suggested we use Tchien as the staging point to explore the countryside.

When the three of us arrived in Gbanga, no carriers were available. In desperation Dean and I concluded that we needed the help of the district commissioner. I introduced myself to him and asked his assistance, using the letter of President Tubman as introduction. The district commissioner said that he would see what he could do. We had to wait a long time before a soldier was sent into town and told to round up any men who were not doing anything and bring them to the compound, the official residence of the district commisioner. When the soldier came back with ten men, the district commissioner said, "Here are your men, and if you have any trouble, take their clothing and then they will have to follow you." I told the men, in the presence of the district commissioner, that we would go to Tchien and the wages they would receive at the end of the journey. The pay was based on the rates in Monrovia and therefore very good for that area. Then we took off. We reached the first village along the road and stayed there overnight. A few times, Dean and I were forced to exercise arm-twisting methods to get enough carriers to maintain the schedule. This was not at all pleasant, but I had to weigh the use of strong-arm tactics against travelling slower, losing valuable time and getting caught up in the rainy season.

After five days we reached Tchien. Four men refused to carry their load the last hour into town. Dean and I told them that they would be paid that day, but we were not going to bribe them with double pay, which was what they were after. To everybody's surprise, Dean, John and I took their loads and carried these into town. Later that afternoon, the four men drifted into town. I decided to provide them with the promised food and later paid them their wages, but docked them for the last day. I did not want any trouble in the crew. The other men were satisfied with this treatment and stayed on the whole expedition, returning with us to Gbanga.

There was a sizeable Christian mission in Tchien. I talked extensively with one of the missionaries and he told me that there was good cooperation between the Christian missions of different denominations of which there were many. This cooperation eliminated conflicting services. It made me think that the ecumenical movement might have started by missionaries. The missionaries felt successful if they could bring the Ten Commandments to the people. Their main effort seemed to be through schooling the young generation. The boarding schools were bunk-houses, separated for boys and girls. The children were dressed in nice white clothes. The missionaries told me they felt the best way to educate their pupils was intern, away from their families and away from their tribal surroundings and influence. I was not sure this was a good idea, because after three or four years the pupils were sent back home. I could imagine the cultural shock for these girls, after being Christian-educated, returning to a communal mud hut. Many must have left home for more civilized jobs, ending up in Monrovia, where there was little work and a high chance of ending up as prostitutes.

The missionaries were helpful to us in other ways. On their advice, Dean hired a headman, who served as interpreter, along with four other men. In return we took along the mail for the Putu mission, when we moved to the known iron deposit in the Putu Range,

Moving on from Tchien we stayed in villages and slept in mud huts. In the beginning it was difficult to obtain food, although there seemed to be enough in this area. Dean solved the problem by taking the food and paying the town chief later, a practise which was accepted. One day we arrived in a village and found that all the people had left. Usually we would arrive and out of all the huts would come children and women and then the men. We wondered if this was a sign of hoping the expedition would move on to the next town. It was already late afternoon and getting stuck, Dean occupied a hut and took three chickens. Suddenly there were ten men standing around him, very upset yelling that these chickens were not his. There, in the middle of that town was Dean, standing authoritatively looking at the men. He had one chicken under his arm and John stood happily beside him with the two other chickens. He waited for the men to stop yelling. When Dean got their attention, he said, through our interpreter, that we would pay for the chickens and if they would bring three other chickens, they would get these back. The other three chickens quickly appeared and were paid for. The town chief agreed to let Dean occupy the hut. Everyone seemed satisfied.

The people were surprised when we paid for the food and lodgings and then they were happy. The slogan, "White man always pay," started to work and after a week in the district, we were getting food and accommodations easily.

We first went to the iron deposit in the Putu Range. I spent a few days analyzing the iron deposit. Dean did the preparatory work so that I could measure the outcrop, take magnetometer readings and collect samples. It was a low grade and low tonnage deposit, with a small seam of high grade iron ore. It was not economical.

In Putu we brought the mail to the mission and stayed there. Two lady missionaries were building an airstrip with their mission children. They wanted technical advice for this project. The clearing was progressing, but the terrain was quite hilly. The amount of earth necessary to remove to make an acceptable, level landing strip was mind-boggling, given their resources. How could I tell this to these two enterprising women? I asked why this project had been started in the first place. One of these women was in bad health and over sixty-five years old. She had arrived in this mission some twenty years earlier and now was supposed to retire. But the American congregation that supported the mission, could not find anyone to replace her. She felt that her services were needed by these children and if there was no replacement, then she was morally obliged to carry on. However, she realized that perhaps one day she would have to be airlifted out of the mission. The mission services in Monrovia had only a water plane, called "Flying Jesus." The airstrip situation was intractable. It was hard to be optimistic and I suggested they investigate another, more level alternative. But they were determined to continue. I never found out how this was resolved.

In the same district there were many gold creeks, all extremely rich in alluvial gold. Dean panned fast and accurate samples. Because of the labour shortage, I saw women working in the creeks, digging the overburden and panning for gold. It seemed worthwhile to explore this area more closely.

We stopped in a village of ten huts. The town chief made a chicken coop, a kind of a lean-to, available for me. One family vacated their hut and moved in with others. That hut was for my carriers. I did not realize that the chicken coop was actually used by half a dozen goats. The goats had been moved into the palaver house. During the middle of the night, a leopard sneaked into town, killed one of the goats and carried it off into the mountains. Here I made a mistake. I should have paid the townspeople for the loss of the goat. I had given Dean our rifle and he suggested hunting the leopard. Dean told me that when a leopard killed a person, it discovered that people were easy prey and it would go then after others. If one person was killed, then all the hunters in the area must get together to hunt down that leopard, because the elders realized that if the leopard was not killed, other people would be killed. It was either kill or be killed.

I felt lucky to not have been quartered in that palaver house that night. It was the usual place offered to valued visitors and one which I would have gladly accepted.

Moving from town to town, we continued prospecting the creeks. In the centre of the next big town was a huge tree, with thousands of nesting canaries. Three old men sat under the tree, each holding a canary with a long string tied to one of its legs. The birds had broken legs from being constantly jerked by the string. Every time they were ready to settle down, they were forced to fly again. These birds were shrieking in pain from this sheer torture. It was horrible to watch. With the interpreter, I went up to these men and asked them why they were treating these birds in this way.

Apparently, the canaries were eating the rice crop and these three birds were being used to frighten away the birds in the tree. I asked the men why they did not cut down that tree, so the birds could not nest there. But they said the tree had always been there and no way would they cut it down. I realized it would be impossible to change their thinking.

The following day south of Tchien we walked through a village in mid-morning. The town chief was in the palaver house with two hunters, who had a little chimpanzee, the size of my fist. It might not have been more than one day old. In the early morning they had shot a big monkey for meat. When the monkey fell out of the tree, this little monkey climbed down out of the tree and settled on the body of the dead mother. The hunters grabbed it. Having heard that in Monrovia the market price of a live monkey was twenty-five dollars, they figured that any white man in the area would pay the same amount. I counter-offered three dollars, but while offering this, I thought, "What do I do with a monkey?" I had heard these animals were good watchmen and were quite intelligent. The American embassy had a chimpanzee that opened the door and accepted letters, but did not allow anybody to enter when no staff was present. It seemed worth the try. Their answer was that three dollars was not enough; they wanted twenty-five dollars. I explained to them that to travel to and from Monrovia would cost more than twenty-five dollars on food alone. I thought three dollars was enough. But no, they wanted twenty-five dollars. I told them that was too bad but then there was no deal. I certainly did not need a monkey on this trip. We moved on and I did not think about it any more.

We continued prospecting, while the crew moved on to the next village. John and I followed slowly. Around noon I heard footsteps and the two hunters caught up to us with the monkey in their hands. They had discussed the journey to Monrovia and concluded that, indeed, it would cost them more, plus there were risks involved in keeping the monkey alive. They offered the monkey for three dollars and there I stood in the middle of the bush with a baby monkey in my hand. As an optimist, I saw no problem. At that time I did not know that the baby had diarrhea, very likely an additional reason to sell the monkey before it died.

I told John to look after the monkey. But was I ever wrong. He refused, saying, "No boh, ugly, jus li mah" (no boss, ugly, just like man). I had to look after the animal myself. The baby monkey was hungry and I took a banana, chewed it fine and then pushed the mush into the monkey's mouth. That worked. Then I figured that the only way I could get the monkey to be accepted was to make the people around her want to be involved.

For three days I carried that monkey and fed her, until we reached the Tchien mission, where I could buy powdered milk and a baby bottle. There we weighed her, she was four hundred and fifty grams. She had black hair, brown eyes and light brown skin. I told John to weave a basket for the night. The first day she had diarrhea, but that disappeared the second day. By this time people wanted to touch her, but I did not allow this. I still had not decided on her name. I was reading a book by Emile Zola, and the attractive lady in this part of his novel had the name of Nana. It sounded all right. Nana it was from then on.

After a week, and as a favour, John was allowed to give the baby her bottle. Now he looked really pleased, but nobody else was yet allowed to touch her. Since I kept Nana in my lap or on my arm most of the day, she was more accepted. I noticed that the locals were coming to watch when I travelled through town with a monkey. She gained quite some strength in her fingers, which was needed to hold on. The first days she laid in my lap, with big eyes quietly looking around. When I fed her milk, she leaked in my lap, but after about ten days, that did not happen any more. She grabbed my leg when I sat down and again when I stood up. She held onto my leg and swung with the rhythm as I walked. It was fun to see how her hands tried to grab things around her, and slowly she started to control these movements. She watched the world around her with her big eyes and once in a while she took off, but suddenly looked around and ran back to me.

After three weeks of prospecting, we left the Tchien district on our way home. On the second day of the return trip, it started to rain. I got very cold, because my clothing was wet inside from sweating and outside from the rain dripping from leaves and branches. All our carriers felt cold. Then the trails became slippery and eventually puddles formed. The rain kept falling and the trails became brooks and at last little streams. We could not see the roots and rocks on the trail due to the muddy water.

The travelling got slower and slower. Dean arranged for local guides who knew the road. And the only way to stay together was to hold the shoulder of the man in front with one hand and use the other hand for balancing, sometimes with the water up to our chests. Our carriers still had their loads on their heads. We came to the crossing of the Cess River, which was usually a quiet floating river. Now it was a dangerous, fast-moving, turbulent current more than three times its normal width. The ferryman could not handle this alone, but needed two extra ferrymen to paddle the canoe across the torrent.

Dean and I kept pushing ahead, until we reached the town of Gbanga. What had been a five day walk in had taken us eight days on the return. We paid off the crew and thanked them for their work. Then we hired a truck. Late that night we arrived in Monrovia, where I was dropped off at the company guest-house. The next morning the guests were surprised to find a monkey crawling in the house and this assured my popularity.

This reconnaissance expedition had been a long shot and it produced no results. It dispelled the hope of finding an economical iron-ore body, but confirmed the widespread occurrences of gold. The last eight strenuous days had overshadowed the expedition. We were worn out. John had come through as a passable cook. Dean had proven to be a natural leader and our safe return was greatly due to his organizational talent and attitude. Surprisingly Nana had survived the travel without a problem. Dean, John and I became a close team.

Life at the Home Base

In our absence superintendent Beuken built a "laboratory," a mud hut about four by ten square metres. Now we had our own office. While I was gone to the Tchien district, Theo had replaced Beuken, who left on furlough to Holland. When I moved back to Bomi Hills, I stayed there for the next three months of the rainy season. Like the first rainy season, this turned out quite differently than anticipated.

I had to organize the laboratory first. The drilling cores had to be stored on racks, the rock samples of our expeditions sorted on trays. Then I made a glass model of the ore body, based on the drilling results from 1938. We had chemicals and laboratory equipment, enabling us to do chemical analysis of the iron ore and to establish the value of the phosphorus and sulphur impurities. For these tasks we needed a sensitive scale and additional laboratory equipment. The company ordered two scales, one extra as a back-up. When the crates arrived, I decided that, in view of the value and the sensitivity of the scales, I better unpack them myself.

In the morning, I went to the laboratory, cleared the counter, and unpacked the first scale. The supply company, K & E, had done an excellent job. Inside the crate was a second crate and inside the second crate was a sealed lead box. The lead box was packed with wood-shavings, shielding a third crate with the sensitive scale packed inside it in paper.

In the afternoon I repeated the unpacking procedure for the second scale: the outside crate, the second crate, the leaden box. For this one I needed a burner to melt the solder. When I was half-way through the second seam, there was a sudden puff, a spontaneous explosion and a fire started inside the box. I closed the box to starve the fire of oxygen, but the fire kept burning. I opened the box again and grabbed at the burning shavings, but the fire got even worse, though there were almost no shavings left. Then, when I started to gain on the fire, one of my helpers in the lab took a bucket of water and, without hesitation, threw the water on the fire. I grabbed the last burning shavings from the fire out of the box. My hands were burnt. Anxiously I cleaned the mess, stripped off the next crate and saw the scale in its full glory. But, the box had received a severe jolt. After careful checking and rechecking against the first scale, I convinced myself, that the second scale was all right. After this harrowing experience, I went home to seek solace with Nana.

Over the last three months, Nana had grown like a weed. It was funny to see her crawl on her four hands. First, she got teeth and then her molars came through. Seeing her trying to walk was really funny. Her legs were too long and her head seemed to be top-heavy, causing her to fall forward, when she tried to walk. When that happened, she rolled over and landed on her back, got mad and yelled like crazy.

Nana, six months old

During the day, when I worked in the office, Nana was alone quite a bit and amused herself. If she got hold of a towel, it seemed to satisfy her need for security. Her curiosity kept her busy. She enjoyed chasing the chickens and when she got mad, she screamed loudly. John and Jimmy spent quite some time with her and took her to the kitchen, where she burned herself and had a nasty blister.

I figured I better teach Nana some facts of life, the first one being how to get her own food. When I had dinner, I put a banana on a table some distance away. She quickly ran to the table, climbed up the leg, got on top of the table and ate the banana. A week later I forgot to put the banana there. When I got my dinner, Nana ran to the table and crawled on top, did not find anything there and slid down and facing me with her big questioning eyes, settled beside me. I asked John for a banana for the table and immediately she climbed to the top, ate the banana, then slid down and took another leg and climbed to the top again, but did not find another banana, looked at me and slid down, then climbed the third leg and again found nothing. I felt sorry for her and quickly got her a banana when she started to climb the fourth leg. After that she was constantly climbing up all the legs of the table. If one did not give her results, there were three other possibilities. It was too bad I did not have enough bananas for all her efforts at that time.

Theo and Hubert each had little boys about two years old, Werner and Jurec. When these boys saw me, they said: "Ugh! Ugh!" which meant they wanted to see Nana.

Cor Immink with Werner and Morliba with Jurec
In the background to the right, the company hotel

I had to go to Monrovia for ten days. It was not convenient to take Nana along. When I returned, the moment she saw me, she screamed and screamed and ran towards me. I noticed how much she had grown, John had looked after her well.

One day she sat in my lap and played with my wristwatch. Suddenly, she grabbed at my pant and got hold of a grasshopper, the size of my thumb. She looked at it, then quickly bit off the grasshopper's head. She seemed to like it and then quietly ate the whole grasshopper, piece by piece. When finished, she looked again at my watch and tried to stop the second hand with no success. Then she started to pull the hairs out of the skin of my hand. She was really enjoying herself and let out satisfied noises.

Nana was very curious and wanted to touch anything that I had in my hands, like pencils or cigarettes. After five months I still had a serious problem. I was unable to house-train her. She would relieve herself on the porch. A little later she would drag her banana through this mess and then continue to eat the banana— very unappetizing to me. Nana did not seem to notice or care about it.

Every morning Nana crawled up the back of my chair and looked to see if the porridge was already there. She knew we would get her a plate too. Further, she would eat three or four bananas a day. In the house she had a preference for the laundry basket and enjoyed hiding in it. When I had visitors, she ran towards me and crawled up my pant leg. When Nana felt like exploring, she looked for her towel, which became her inseparable partner. She might take off on an expedition of her own. She once reached the hotel across the road, taking the towel along.

I took Nana on the next expedition, north of the concession, close to Bomi Hills.

Preparation for an expedition, Nana on my back
John dressed in white

She travelled in one of the boxes with the supplies. If she thought that the carriers were not treating her right, she would grab a branch and hang there, loudly yelling and then the crew had to catch her.

When we returned from this expedition, there were some guests in the hotel and I visited them. Around the corner came Nana, announcing her presence: "Ugh! Ugh! Ugh! Ugh!" She ran towards the leg of our general manager, grabbed his trouser leg and settled there. The general manager had indicated earlier that he was annoyed with the monkey, but I noticed that he seemed to like being the chosen saviour.

Not being under pressure to work out notes, I had time to talk to the local crew. One Saturday afternoon I was waiting for a parcel that the Brewerville warehouse was sending me by pick-up truck. It was to arrive mid-afternoon. I moved outside to the road and sat there on a fallen tree, waiting for the truck to arrive. It was payday. A group of labourers passed by and said: "Hello boh, how aw you."

"Fine, what do you have in your pocket?" I asked.

"A paper, boh."

"Show me" I said and they handed me the paper. It was: *Time* magazine, dated October 1939.

"What did you pay for this?" I asked.

"Turty cent, boh"

"Can you read?"

"No boh."

"Shall I read for you?"

"Yes, boh."

So they all settled on the tree beside me, but before I started to read, I asked the man why he had bought the magazine?

"Because of the pictures," he said.

I read to them about Roosevelt, then quite a story about Italy, Cordell Hull and Brindisi. A huge grasshopper jumped on the paper. I shoved it off and thought, sure enough, they don't understand a thing of what I am reading to them, but the owner of the paper said every so often: "Oh goo!" " Sooo!" "You hea!"

Suddenly the truck, I had been waiting for, stopped beside us. I collected the parcel and I told the men that I had to go, leaving them with the magazine with pictures.

The next day was Sunday. With three new staff members from Holland, Hubert and I were sitting relaxed on the porch, talking. Nana had settled on my lap. The head carpenter and two of his friends passed my hut. They were experienced carpenters, very tall people, and good to work with. The company had hired them from Nigeria. They worked six days a week and on the seventh day, they partied. Today they were in a good mood and it was no wonder. They showed us a bottle of gin and asked if we recognized it. Of course we did! The head carpenter said, "I drink this in one glass, the whole bottle."

"Really?"

"Yes, white men sip and sip, drink and drink in small glasses, smoke and smoke, talk and talk. That is wasting time."

I thought, that was quite a philosophical statement about getting drunk fast.

Since our company provided steady employment, the people had more money and were able to pay the dowry for a woman. This was between twenty and forty dollars. The men usually told me when they had 'bought' a wife and I would invite the man to show me the woman. They were hoping for that, because then I would give her a dash.

One of our men came with a girl of about twelve years old. I told him that she was far too young for him. He said, "Oh, it does not bother me, in a few years she will be old enough." In the meantime, he slept with his present wife and this girl in the same bed. The girl looked very proud and happy to be his future wife.

Then one day John told me he had taken a wife. He had bought her for twenty dollars. "Oh Boh, she's fai e fe" (Oh boss, she is fine and fat). Later I was introduced to her.

We celebrated the second Christmas quietly in Bomi Hills with the families Immink and Viola and a new foreman. The weekend before I had visited the Firestone plantation, where some other Dutchmen were employed, who partied and drank heavily. Then I realized that, at Bomi Hills, we were a sedate set of people.

For the New Year's party that year, all the families from Bomi Hills went to Brewerville. The truck road was now completed and this time we all drove in two hours to the company compound in Brewerville, where we had a sentimental celebration.

New Year's Day 1950 was the centennial celebration of Liberia and an official holiday. There would be a parade in Monrovia with the Home Guard followed by the volunteer army. We decided to go and watch. The Home Guard, well-dressed, marched smartly at the head of the parade. The volunteer army was sad and funny. Half of the column was barefooted and most of the participants were out of step. The officer, who led the column, walked with his sabre unsheathed, but was so drunk that he did not realize that he was marching slowly off the road. Eventually he laid down in the grass, still singing loudly. Another soldier went over to him, took his sabre and belt, put the belt on and continued at the head of that column. Although it was a funny sight, it was also very sad for the image of the army.

Two weeks later was the official opening of the truck road from Monrovia to Bomi Hills. This was to show the Liberians what progress meant. We all assisted in the organization to make this opening a success.

Our president invited Liberian officialdom, as well as dignitaries of the foreign services: the President of Liberia, Mr Tubman, all the ministers, all the envoys, the senate members, the members of parliament, the district commissioners, our clan chief and our town chief, all were there. First we had a quiet lunch on the porch of my hut, the only sizeable room available. It was attended by President Tubman and his assistant, our company president, the general manager, Mr Beuken, Theo and myself.

In early afternoon about two hundred and fifty guests arrived in more than forty cars. The company had organized a taxi service of jeeps to transport the officials to the top of Bomi Hills and back, for whom ever wanted to see that. In the company hotel, the mud hut opposite my hut, there were sandwiches and drinks. I was assigned to the bar.

During the party, I encountered the most unexpected situations. My own labourers were walking among the parliamentarians. One coming over, telling me, "that one is my uncle and that one also." I saw others grabbing into the cigar boxes, one man trying to smoke a cigar still wrapped in a cellophane paper. Others were grabbing sandwiches from the plates. To me it looked like pandemonium.

I was told that the President's drink was bourbon, the American whiskey. Because the President drank bourbon, others wanted that too and I soon ran out. I thought, "whiskey is whiskey," and I made a nice Scotch drink. After serving this to the President, our company president came running into the bar:

"What have you done? Are you poisoning the President?"

I told him about my predicament and how I figured that I solved it. At that time I did not know the difference between Scotch and bourbon, coming from Holland where there was neither Scotch nor bourbon. The President had to settle for the Scotch and was not very happy.

Later that afternoon President Tubman was introduced to the clan chief, the town chief and to one of our native overseers. He then gave a speech to all the guests. Afterwards, everybody got back into their cars for the ride back. But one car did not have enough gas to make it back, so we filled its tank. Of course, after that, every car had to be topped up. Fortunately we had some seven 45-gallon drums with gas on the property and after topping up all the cars, the party drove off.

By 5 p.m. all was quiet again.

Expeditions with Two Geologists

Early in 1950 our company president brought in two American geologists to advise him on the merits of the exploration potential of the concession. Theo and I went to Brewerville to meet them. One of them, Dr. T. P. (Tom) Thayer, had been the geological expert in the infant stages of the U.S. Economic Mission in 1943 in Monrovia and at that time had visited Bomi Hills. He had also served as our president's adviser during Republic Steel's visit six months earlier. This time when Tom visited the U.S. Economic Mission, he found out about the aerial survey, that had been done during the war, but also learned that the pictures were all mixed up in boxes. The flight plans were missing, the "key" was lost. He loaded the boxes of photographs into a jeep and brought them to Brewerville to see what could be done. He secured a bungalow that was under construction. The floor, walls and roof were up, the windows and doors were installed. It was just an empty shell, ideal for sorting thousands of pictures. For a few days I worked with Tom. The photographs had been taken at a constant altitude in strips on a south-to-north flight, followed by a return flight from the north to south. Each strip was numbered and each photograph on each strip had a sequential number. All strips started or ended at the coast. Every photograph overlapped the previous one by about three quarters and each strip overlapped the previous strip by about the same amount.

We started with the pictures of the bay of Monrovia, which we recognized. From there we were able to line up a section of the coast. While Tom and the U.S. Economic Mission people were making contacts and arrangements with the officials from the foreign affairs, economics and mining departments, I continued with the sorting and matching of the pictures and became fascinated. I got addicted to this puzzle, spending up to fourteen hours a day trying to match the pictures. The main guide was the coastline and because I had travelled quite a bit in the Interior, I recognized a number of the towns, which was helpful. It was noticeable that slight variations were caused by side winds during these flights. I plotted the flights on a map of Liberia and from then on, we could pinpoint the photos for the area we needed. The "key" to the pictures was solved and completed in ten days. However, there was a problem with the pictures. About eighty kilometres inland from the coast, the strips of photos showed an increase of overlap towards the centre, as if the plane had drifted off course. We discussed the possibilities. Was this drift because of side wind? It did not seem likely to be that much. Or could it be that the pilots, got fed up with the job in such a faraway country, wanted to return home as soon as possible? It never occurred to us that this excessive drift of the planes had to do with an abnormally high magnetic deviation in that area.

Some ten years later a Swedish geologist went to the north and discovered an enormous iron ore deposit that straddled the border and continued deep into French Guinea. That huge deposit was what caused the abnormally high magnetic deviation. It was eventually developed for production. We had underestimated the professional competence of the photographic department of the U.S. Air Force. It was a real blunder to have jumped to a conclusion and not to have thoroughly analyzed all the possibilities. This was the most costly geological mistake of my life.

In the meeting with the American geologists for the planning of the expeditions, Jordense was present, as he had travelled into and had quite some knowledge of the hinterland of Liberia. It was decided that first we would review the work that Theo and I had done. This would take about one month and Jordense was going to join us. After that we would go, on Jordense's suggestion, to the Zorzor district in the northern part of the Western Province of Liberia. This was outside our concession. It would involve another three to four weeks. This area was accessible only by using the truck road into French Guinea and then circling back west to the northern part of Liberia's Western Province.

A new problem entered our world. The Americans were worried about schistosomiasis. We had never heard of the disease. They explained that it was caused by a parasitic worm in a complicated life cycle that could be picked up in fresh water and involved snails. When the worm penetrated the body in the blood stream, it could nestle itself in the bladder and in the next stage, it could penetrate the liver. The disease was extremely painful, especially when relieving. All we could find out was that there was a cure, but it took six months. The geologists told us not to wade through creeks and to have the wash water boiled, as well as the laundry. The table conversations centered around how to prevent this illness. Theo and I must have been extremely lucky not to be affected so far, but from then on we took the precautions they advised.

Before we left, we had a session with our stewards, cooks and laundry men about the health requirements in relation to schistosomiasis. All drinking water and all the laundry had to be boiled and the handling of these requirements were discussed.

We selected the photo strips for the area of the expedition to the sites, which Theo and I had discovered. Travelling in the Interior and having these arial photos with the overlap gave us a three dimensional view of the countryside. It was a real improvement in geological extrapolation.

We required equipment and supplies for the five of us and it ended up that we needed sixty carriers. Dean was in charge of this expedition and he ran it efficiently. Our American geologists were so impressed with his performance that they brought his salary up to the European standard. This made Dean one of the best paid Liberian employees and I was glad for him.

Expedition with sixty carriers for four geologists

Four weeks later we were at Theo's tourmaline gold deposit. One day we returned to the camp around midday. When crossing the creek near the camp, we noticed one of the laundry men rinsing our clothing in the creek. We asked the laundry man if he would boil the clothes afterwards and he said that he had already boiled our clothing, it needed only to be rinsed, dried and folded. We were shocked and I asked if this was the procedure. The laundry man said that since the first day, this was the way he did it. Apparently he had followed the instructions blindly, not understanding the disinfecting aspect of the boiling, and the rinsing was not mentioned by one of us. We hoped that none of us was infected with schistosomiasis. Theo and I made sure that the procedure was corrected and in the following days we checked the handling of the laundry.

That night, Tom noticed that his trunk had been forced open and his money taken out. In its place was a dirty, bundled handkerchief and, inside, a good helping of fried ants. I never saw Tom explode so badly. He was furious at his steward for not watching his trunk more closely. Theo and I had known the steward for more than a year and we were sure he could be trusted. But we never found the culprit.

On the way back to Bomi Hills our party camped on the trail between Bambona and Bambuta, revisiting the iron outcrops that Theo and I had evaluated a year earlier. The crew wanted to stay in one of the nearby towns and that was all right with us.

In the middle of the night, some men travelled through the campsite and took about fifty pieces of clothing, some shoes and an aluminum folding chair. The next morning our stewards realized what had happened. Our returning crew had met strangers on the trail. Dean headed off in that direction. The thieves could only follow trails and there were none in this bush, except the ones between the towns. The bush itself was impregnable and could only be travelled through slowly, using cutlasses. Going from one town to the next, in late afternoon Dean caught up with three strangers in a sizeable town. The town chief was willing to handcuff one stranger and by assisting in the interrogation, Dean was able to extract a confession from this man, compromising the other two. The second man was also handcuffed, but the third man disappeared into the bush. The local people were confident that he would eventually be caught, as the whole district was aware of the theft.

The following day the two prisoners revealed where they had hidden their loot. They knew they eventually would be caught so they had cut up all the clothing and it was useless. The clan chief requested that Dean deliver the two prisoners to the district commissioner in Clay, as it was in the same direction that our party would travel on our way back to Bomi Hills. That night, two soldiers with the two prisoners came to our camp. The treatment of the prisoners was harsh. Their heads were shaved and their bodies were smeared with mud. The population and the soldiers handled them roughly, spitting at them as they passed. They were made to carry a heavy load towards the district commissioner's town and I learned that the punishment very likely would be hard labour for eighteen months.

Back in Monrovia we organized the following expedition to the northern part of the Western Province around Zorzor. We rented three trucks and took the road north-east into French Guinea. The two American geologists and the director of mines, a graduate of the Colorado School of Mines, were in a pick-up truck. Our truck, like most other trucks in Liberia, had the front doors removed and replaced by a wooden seat over the full width of the truck, which stuck out on both sides of the cabin. This provided sitting room for seven people, with two men on each side sitting outside the cabin. In the back of the truck were our supplies with twenty carriers riding on top. The third truck was similar and Dean was in charge of it. On the main highway, some five hundred kilometres from Monrovia, a few hours past Gbanga, on a winding section of the road, the steering pin fell out and our truck veered into the ditch and turned over. Miraculously, only one man was hurt. Fifty kilometres up the road was a mission with the only doctor in a radius of a few hundred kilometres. Tom organized the help and took the injured man to the mission. He recovered in three days, while the truck was being repaired.

We travelled through French Guinea, where the gravel roads were in good shape. We re-entered Liberia and reached Zorzor, the seat of the paramount chief of the Bussy tribe. In Zorzor there was also a Lutheran mission and the school, where Dean had been educated. Dean introduced me to his mother and that was very moving for me. I felt helpless because I could not think of a worthwhile present in my trunk. I did not think that tobacco leaves were appropiate.

We investigated areas in the surrounding countryside, suggested by Jordense, but there was no indication of something of interest to follow up on. After three weeks we returned to Monrovia empty-handed.

The American geologists left for home.

A few weeks later the rainy season started. It was the third and last year of our contract and we could not do any prospecting for a period of six months. The company decided that we had better go on furlough and return in October.

Theo and I headed to Bomi Hills to pack our bags.

The End of my Stay in Liberia

Back in Bomi Hills, Theo and I stored the equipment in the laboratory and cleaned the office. We made arrangements for our crew to be incorporated with Beuken's work. There were new staff employees who needed a cook and a steward. Jimmy and John were able to choose their new employer. We said goodbye to the Beuken and Viola families.

I left Bomi Hills one day ahead of the Immink family travelling in the company jeep. It was a pleasure to drive the two hours to Monrovia, instead of travelling three days on foot, as we had to the first time. I stopped half-way at the sawmill to say good-bye. The sawmill produced the railroad ties from local sources for our railroad track. The sawmill superintendent was sitting behind his desk. Through the window he could keep an eye on the operation, where seven men were working.

It was quite a different sight from two years earlier, when the sawmill started up. At that time there were three superintendents, a Scotsman, an Englishman and a Dutchman, and about twenty five locals, all trying to get the sawmill going. The diesel engine, a Buda, was bought second-hand. The engine was designed for water-cooling, but in this bush there was no water around. None of the men had worked in a sawmill before. You could imagine the yelling and blaming that went on at this operation. The whole organization had to get into a routine: the supplying of the trees, the sawing, the storing of the railroad ties, the maintenance of the mill and eventually the distribution of the finished product.

When I arrived in Monrovia, I had to find a home for Nana. When I got Nana, I had realized that there would be a problem when I would leave Liberia. Nana had not learned to fend for herself in the jungle. Taking Nana with me, I would be faced with a three months quarantine in Rotterdam, which was not good for both of us. I had made sure that Nana was not attached to one person. Then I heard of a Danish couple, both biologists, who bought monkeys for zoos. I asked if they were interested in taking Nana. They asked how much that would cost. I told them that if they looked after her well, she would be theirs. They invited me to their house and over dinner we talked about the details. I felt satisfied that she would be well looked after. The next day Nana and I parted on their doorstep. I had become attached to her.

We got our airplane tickets in the office and that evening Cor, Theo and I were invited to Jordense's home after dinner. It was a balmy evening and we were sitting on the balcony, enjoying the ocean breeze. We were served drinks and slowly the stories started to flow. Jordense began to tell about his experience in the early thirties, his first year in Liberia, at the crossing of the Loffa River.

I could remember it vividly myself.

It must have been the first or the second time I had gone on expedition alone with my crew. That morning we started early and we reached the Loffa River at mid-morning. It was huge, reminding me of the Rhine with the water flowing steady and smoothly. A canoe lay on the other side of the river with no ferryman in sight. I was soaked with perspiration and the water looked so inviting and cool that I suggested I swim across and pick up the canoe. My foreman, as well as my cook and all the others, were against me doing this. They talked loudly, explaining why I should not go. My English was still rudimentary and I was not yet used to pidgin English. They followed me to the edge of the river. I got undressed, they kept urging me not to go. Without listening I jumped into the river. I had to watch the current. Half-way across I realized it was farther than I had thought, but I was in good shape and never felt I was in danger. After a good twenty to thirty minutes I reached the other side, picked up the canoe and paddled back. We then ferried the crew. When we passed through the village of the ferryman, we paid him for the use of the canoe and continued our travel. Jordense told much the same story. But in his version, the river was filled with crocodiles. Apparently when his friend was half-way across, a crocodile showed up, swimming between him and his friend. He did not dare to shoot as the bullet might ricochet over the surface of the water and hit his friend. Yelling did not help, as he was too far away. He saw his friend being pulled under water and disappear. For a long time after this story we sat very still. I realized then that my foreman must have said there were crocodiles in the river, but I had not understood his pidgin English at that time and did not listen to him. I also now realized what kind of predicament I had put upon my crew, as they felt responsible for me. And last but not least, I realized how fortunate I had been that there were no crocodiles nearby.

The next morning the company car drove us to the Liberian International Airport in Robertsville. This time we boarded a Constellation on our way home.

The one thing that I did not miss on leaving was the tropical heat. Flying back in comfort high above the ocean, I thought of all the good people I had worked with and the loyalty and security they had given me: Jimmy, my cook; Daniel, my hunter-headman; Dean and John's friendship. I wondered about Nana, how would she make out.

These two years had been a wonderful experience and left me with many cherished memories.

Epilogue

After leaving Liberia in May 1950, I returned to Holland and spent a few months travelling around the country, seeing old friends and meeting new ones. Thinking about what to do next, I decided to see more of the world. Over the years I heard lots of interesting stories about South America. The head offices of the mining companies were in New York, so I took the boat to New York and started job-hunting.

Early September on a sunny day during the lunch hour, I was walking on the busy sidewalk of Wall Street when I ran into our company president. The last time we had met was four months earlier in Monrovia. We were surprised to see each other and he asked what I was doing there. I told him I was hunting for a job in South America. He invited me to come to his office that afternoon and, after some discussion, it was arranged that I would go back to Liberia for three months. Together with Theo, I would complete the investigation of a deposit that looked intriguing. I returned immediately to Holland with the intention of later returning to New York to continue looking for a job.

Prior to my boat trip from Rotterdam to New York, I had met a student, Hanneke, who I had asked to marry me. After the war it was still very hard to get a visa to enter certain countries, if you did not have a job, particularly the United States. As an employee of the Liberia Mining Company I had no problem and as my wife, Hanneke could join me in the U.S. It was impossible to arrange our marriage before my departure to Liberia. Because of this time limitation, the simplest solution was to get married by proxy, which in Holland is called "the wedding with the glove." Holland is one of the few countries where a proxy marriage is possible. Only the queen or king can grant permission. The practise was used in the nineteenth and twentieth century by employees who worked in the Dutch East and West Indies and who could receive free passage for their fiancee only if they were married. The use of the glove, to indicate commitment, goes back to the Middle Ages. This time, my fiancee, Hanneke had to request special permission from Queen Juliana of The Netherlands. Before leaving Holland, my personal arrangements were still up in the air. I gave my brother power of attorney and asked him to be my representative at the wedding. I also gave him my right-hand glove, while I took along the left-hand glove as a symbolic sign.

At the beginning of November, Theo and I left for Liberia and were waved goodbye by Cor and Hanneke.

Upon reaching Bomi Hills it was good to see Dean, John and Jimmy and to find the crew reasonably intact. We got ready for the next expedition, took off and after some six days travel we reached our destination. There we started the work.

At night Theo teased me about my status, "Are you married now?" It started to annoy me and eventually, after a month, I had a premonition that December twelfth should be my wedding day, so I took the day off. Theo said that he thought it was a waste of time and got ready for work. He took his notebook and water bottle, checked the crew and the tools and left. A few minutes later he returned, took off his gear and said that he ought to give me moral support on this very important day. We got the folding chairs and the bridge table ready. I had taken a bottle of sherry along for when I received the telegram that I was married, but it seemed the right time to open it now.

Wedding picture with Theo, in the background Willy Beer

I slipped the left-hand glove over the neck of the sherry bottle, then Theo made a wedding picture attended by Willy Beer, our present steward. We opened the bottle and celebrated the day.

Ten days later a carrier from Bomi Hills arrived, with a telegram from Holland with the news that I was married. It was on the very same day that Theo and I celebrated.

At the very same time, the proxy wedding service took place in the townhall of Leyden, The Netherlands. Family and friends were there to support my future wife, Hanneke. The ceremony was similar to a normal wedding. My brother, who represented me, wore my right-hand glove and signed all the papers. My brother's wife with their two year old son sat in the audience, feeling like a fifth wheel. Hanneke related to me that this was not a festive occasion. To her it felt like a cold shower.

Theo and I continued prospecting and stayed another month in the area, investigating all the alluvial deposits and outcrops and mapping the countryside. After completion we travelled along the Loffa River. In one of the tributaries we made test pits and washed for gold and diamonds with encouraging results. We returned to Bomi Hills with the information and made our report.

In Bomi Hills I found a letter from New York with a job offer as chief engineer at the Compania de Huanchaca de Bolivia, a base metal mine high up in the Cordilleras de los Andes in Bolivia. I said goodbye to the people with whom I had spent a few years and left for Monrovia. A week later I flew to New York and met my wife, Hanneke, on our way to South America.

Acknowledgements

The geological treatise of the Liberian country and its economic importance was written by *Ir* Th.W. Immink and presented to the Mining Association - M.V.Delft - printed in 1992 Eeuwboek - M.V. Delft, The Netherlands.

The political, business and commercial side of Bomi Hills was a real poker game. We employees were not aware of our involvement. Our savings, left in the accounts with the company in the New York office, were being used as working capital at these critical times. This side of the story was presented so well by Mr Garland R. Farmer in his article: "About Lansdell K. Christie, The Liberian Ore Industry And Some Related People And Events." It was printed in 1992 Eeuwboek - M.V. Delft, The Netherlands.

Theo and I worked together in the jungle. We got to rely and depend on each other, an experience that continued to this day and that I cherish.

I have to thank many. My thoughts go especially to Theo and Cor Immink and Hubert and Dora Viola, who kept our camp in Bomi Hills, for me, a haven of sanity. These two families always made me feel welcome.

The completion of this manuscript was not possible without the assistance and patience of Jo van der Pot, Jacquiline Lapointe, Les Clarke, my son Reinout and Maria Daw.

I want to thank my editor Ms. Andrea Langlois for helping me organize the manuscript before she left for Africa. I thank Ms. Jill Fallis for completing it. I also wish to acknowledge the efforts of the staff of Trafford Publishing.

Albert Reilingh
Saanichton, B.C

Printed in the United States
by Baker & Taylor Publisher Services